CHOOSING
HIS HAND

Julia Fischer

CHOOSING HIS HAND

JULIA KERCHER

CROSSBOOKS

CrossBooks™
A Division of LifeWay
1663 Liberty Drive
Bloomington, IN 47403
www.crossbooks.com
Phone: 1-866-879-0502

First published by CrossBooks 11/3/2011

ISBN: 978-1-4627-1147-5 (e)
ISBN: 978-1-4627-0562-7 (sc)
ISBN: 978-1-4627-0657-0 (hc)

Library of Congress Control Number: 2011916370

Printed in the United States of America

This book is printed on acid-free paper.

To God, who promised to never leave me,
and to my father, who has also never left me.

PREFACE

Who's in control of your life? You would probably like to think that you are, but you would be wrong. None of us are truly in control. Someone other than ourselves is leading every one of us. The good news is that we get to choose who that "Someone" will be.

We all choose into whose hand we will place our lives. That option remains with us until the day we die. Some make the right choice right away and stick with it. Some make the wrong one and, sadly, are lost forever. Still others make the wrong choice, but eventually come to realize their mistake and make the right one. I fit into that last category.

I chose to place my life in the wrong hand at a young age. That choice led to serious, irreversible consequences. I'm not proud of the choices that I made, but I've chosen to share my journey in hopes that it will help others to not make those same choices.

Everything that you are about to read is true to the best of my recollection. My greatest hope is that everyone who reads this book will know that no matter how far you have strayed away from God, you can be assured that He has not given up on you. His open hand is waiting to welcome you back.

*I give them eternal life, and they shall never perish;
no one can snatch them out of My hand.*—John 10:28 (NIV)

CONTENTS

CHAPTER 1

You are not in control

By the time he was two years old, it was apparent that our eldest son was exceptional. Besides already speaking in full sentences (with correct grammar), Randal scored off the charts in nearly every area on a developmental screening test that assessed children up to the age of six. However, in addition to being exceptionally intelligent, Randal was also exceptionally strong-willed.

At two-and-a-half, our firstborn still refused to use the toilet. It wasn't that he didn't know how, he just didn't want to. Bribes of stickers and candy failed to achieve the outcome we were seeking. We tried putting Randal in cloth diapers, hoping to make him uncomfortable. That plan backfired and served only to make us uncomfortable. We switched back to the highly absorbent disposables and waited for him to decide when it was time for "big-boy underwear"—which he did shortly thereafter.

But the battle was just beginning. Randal simply would not submit to authority anymore than I did at his age. Like me, he seemed to think that he knew better than adults and, therefore, did not have to listen to them. Refusing to obey was his way of trying to be "in control". But his desire to be in control and refusal to operate within guidelines led to some pretty significant consequences, both inside and outside of our home.

In preschool, Randal pushed a classmate off the jungle gym when the boy would not get out of his way. The boy landed on a concrete floor and was hospitalized overnight for a concussion. By first grade, things were not much better. Randal was still having issues with authority and was suspended out of school for two days when he caused a girl to fall face-first down a slide by unhooking her feet from the top. Although the girl shouldn't have been on the slide in that position in the first place, Randal's action was considered "physical aggression" because he already had a reputation for being a bully.

What concerned me the most about Randal was that he didn't seem to feel bad about these incidents. He demonstrated no remorse or true contrition. And not only was he not sorry for the pain he caused his classmates, but he was also not sorry for the pain he caused us with his disobedience and belligerence. He justified his anger by complaining that our consequences were "unfair".

Soon after his suspension, I watched in agony as his father escorted Randal to his room after yet another outburst. It absolutely broke my heart to see his defiance continue. I knew that Randal's choices would lead him down a path that I did not want to see him take. If something didn't change, my son's life would mirror mine—and that thought terrified me.

My life was certainly not one that I wanted any of my children's lives to mirror. My life was a mess and it was all due to one important choice that I made when I was just a little younger than Randal. That choice set me on a path to destruction—the very path that I wanted to save Randal from.

Like Randal, I was taught about God from a young age. My parents took me to church and Sunday School nearly every week. I even went to Vacation Bible School in the summer. But circumstances in my life caused me to begin to doubt the existence of an all-powerful, loving God. The doubt began after my younger sister, Jill, was born. She had visual and developmental impairments that took a lot of my parents' time and attention. I was jealous of that attention and I became resentful of her.

It didn't make sense to me why a loving God would let her be born that way. What did *she* do to deserve that? What did *I* do to deserve that?

My older sister, Janice, also had some health issues when she was young. By the time she entered school, she was doing fine physically, but she was very quiet and withdrawn. She was quite unpopular and got bullied a lot. When I entered school, I was automatically unpopular because I was her sister. It didn't seem fair to be ruthlessly teased and tormented simply because of my last name.

Then came the pivotal point in my life. I was walking home after kindergarten one day when some older girls asked me to come and play with them on a four-person teeter-totter. These were the same girls that usually teased me and called me names, but I didn't question it. I was just grateful for the offer and immediately accepted.

It was early spring and the ground was wet from melting snow. It had been "picture day" at school, so I was wearing snow boots and carried my dress shoes in a paper bag. One of the girls offered to take the bag and set it aside for me as I got on the teeter-totter. This was the first time I'd ever been included with the "popular" kids, and I was on top of the world. I had so much fun. But when it was time to go home, I discovered the real reason for the unexpected invitation.

I walked over to pick up my shoes and saw that the girl had placed the bag in a mud puddle. When I picked it up, the bag fell apart and the shoes tumbled into the mud. I turned around to see the girls pointing and laughing at me. Tears stung my eyes as I grabbed my muddy shoes and ran home.

I couldn't understand how anyone could be so cruel. I was only six years old. I'd never done anything to deserve such treatment. In church and Sunday school I'd been taught that God loves us and takes care of us. Well where was God then? If He loved me, why did He let those girls treat me that way? Why didn't He do something to protect me?

That was when I decided that I couldn't trust anyone anymore, and "anyone" included God. I questioned why God allowed cruelty and why He let other bad things happen. I even began to question His existence.

I attended public school, so I was taught evolution. I was told that the universe is billions (or maybe trillions) of years old and everything evolved out of nothing. I asked my teacher where God came from, but she couldn't answer me, citing "separation of church and state". I didn't know what that meant, but what I did know was that none of what I was learning about God in church seemed to fit with what I was learning in school—and it certainly didn't fit with what I was *experiencing* there.

Some kids at school didn't believe in God. They reasoned there was no *proof* of His existence. Because they couldn't see Him, they decided He must not be there. I didn't understand then how ridiculous that line of thinking really was. I can't see the wind or gravity either, but I know that they exist because I can see and feel their effects. But I didn't think about that at the time.

Instead I thought that I had to choose which adults to believe. I could believe my pastor and Sunday School teachers who said that God created us, we are subject to His authority, and we will be judged by Him one day according to His standards. Or I could choose to believe my public school teacher who said that there is no God, we evolved from apes, and we are ultimately subject only to standards set by humans and have no eternal consequences for our actions.

The choice seemed simple. Feeling guilt for breaking God's law and fearing eternal damnation in Hell didn't sound very good to me. But breaking human-imposed rules had usually resulted in minimal punishment or even no consequences at all. That sounded a lot better. So I chose to turn my back on God, deny His existence, and go my own way. That was the worst choice I ever made. I didn't know it at the time, but I had opened myself up for Satan to grab me.

As I went to Randal's room to talk to him, I reflected on that early decision. I knew I did *not* want him to make that same choice. I wanted to spare him from the decades of pain that I experienced as a result of my attempt to be in control of my own life.

I stood outside Randal's door and paused to pray before opening it. I prayed, "God, please give me the right words to say to him." I then opened the door and found Randal sitting on the floor. He looked so small and vulnerable sitting in the middle of his large room, nothing like the "big kid" he was trying to be. I sat down on the floor in front of him, still not knowing what to say, but feeling an intense desire to steer him in the right direction. As I glanced around the room, I noticed a pair of Randal's shoes lying on the floor. Since he was so bright, I knew Randal would understand the analogy that came to me.

I picked up one of the shoes with my left hand. I explained to Randal, "This shoe can do nothing on its own. It needs someone to move it. Like this shoe, we are powerless on our own."

I put the shoe in my right hand and said, "When we place ourselves in God's hand, He takes control and moves us according to His plan. But if we choose to leave His hand . . ." I dropped the shoe on the floor. "Satan grabs us." I grabbed the shoe again with my left hand. "Then Satan has control of us and moves us according to his will and he will continue to do so until we choose to return to God's hand." I placed the shoe back in my right hand.

"You have to make the choice, Randal. You can be in God's hand, in His control, or you can try to do it on your own and have Satan grab you. No matter what, *you* are not in control."

I put the shoe back on the floor and walked out of the room, closing the door behind me. I stood outside of his door and thanked God for giving me those words. I then prayed that the lesson would sink in and that Randal would make the right choice.

CHAPTER 2

Choosing a hand

Soon after "the shoe lesson", Randal made his choice. He accepted Christ as his Savior and was baptized before completing first grade. Less than two years after that, he was sharing his faith with others.

We were living in Omaha and Randal was in the third grade. Like me, he attended public school. The difference was that he was already grounded in his faith and, therefore, would not succumb to the lie of evolution. Instead he began sharing the truth of the Gospel with his friends at school. He invited one of those friends to spend the night at our home.

When it was time for the boys to go to bed, Randal insisted that Jonah join us for our nightly Bible and prayer time. Jonah was quiet, clearly taking it all in and processing. Randal had been working on him for some time and it seemed that it was all coming together for Jonah and beginning to make sense.

After the boys had been in bed for a while, I walked down the hallway to my room. As I passed Randal's door, I heard talking coming from his room. I prepared to open the door and tell the boys to get to sleep, but stopped when I heard Randal ask Jonah, "Are you ready?"

I heard Jonah reply, "Yes." Tears filled my eyes as I heard Randal recite a prayer of salvation with Jonah repeating his every word. I could not have been more proud of him than I was at that very moment. This boy who, a few years earlier, appeared to be on the path to becoming the next school-shooter was now a school evangelist. He had chosen to place himself in God's hand and, because of that, God was able to use Randal to reach out to Jonah and lead him to salvation in Christ.

Randal made the right choice. I, on the other hand, made the wrong choice. I chose to go my own way in hopes of experiencing freedom. But instead of leading me to freedom, that choice led me to bondage. Satan grabbed me—and he held on tight. He sought to accomplish his will in my life, which was to destroy me. And I went along with nearly everything he wanted me to do.

At the age of nine, I wasn't witnessing to my classmates like Randal. I was taking my first sip of vodka. I was only in the fourth grade, but I was already feeling tremendous pressure to succeed academically. School came fairly easy to me. I didn't have to try very hard to achieve good grades, so my teachers and parents came to expect that from me. But sometimes I failed to live up to their expectations. If I had a report card with all A's and one B, the focus always seemed to be on the one B. I felt as though I was never quite good enough. No matter how hard I tried, I could never attain perfection and I thought that I had to be perfect to gain approval from the adults in my life.

I thought that maybe I wasn't good enough to gain God's approval either. Maybe that was why He let so many bad things happen to me. Many of my classmates were telling me how worthless I was. Continuing to hear that day after day, I started to believe it—and it really hurt. It hurt so much that all I wanted was a way to make the pain go away. I thought that I could find it in my parents' liquor cupboard.

Although my parents didn't drink much, both of their families did and I saw drinking a lot growing up. I recall that every time we visited my mom's dad, he would have a Jack and Coke in his hand. I remember one time accidentally picking up his glass and taking a sip. It was awful. I couldn't even drink Coke for some time after that because it reminded me of the taste of whiskey.

One New Year's Eve, my parents gave me a sip of champagne at midnight. That tasted awful too. I couldn't understand why on earth anyone would want to drink alcohol. It certainly couldn't be for the taste, so there must be some other reason.

Whenever I was around people who were drinking, they always seemed happy. In movies and on TV, I had seen people drinking alcohol to escape pain. I had a lot of pain and I wanted an escape. So I opened the liquor cupboard in search of that escape. My parents entertained often, so there was an assortment to choose from. I found some cherry vodka. Thinking that it might taste like cherry Kool-Aid, I took a sip. It was *nothing* like Kool-Aid so that sip was all I had then.

Not long after that, I found a can of beer in the refrigerator and decided to give that a try. That was even more disgusting. I couldn't believe that people could possibly drink that stuff. Obviously I couldn't just put it back, so I tried flavoring it with some maraschino cherry juice—*not* a good idea. That didn't make it any better. I gave up on the beer and poured it down the drain.

Still, I wouldn't give up. I had to find some way to get enough alcohol in me that I would feel something. I tried mixing all of the different liquors I could find with things like juice, pop, or Kool-Aid. Eventually I accomplished my goal. Finally I was able to drink enough to feel an effect. The constant emotional pain that I felt was lessened, at least for a while.

While I was drunk, I didn't have to think. I didn't like thinking. Thinking was painful because all I thought about was how worthless I was.

Ironically, drinking also gave me a sense of control. I was getting away with doing something I had been told not to do. I wasn't going to let anyone tell me what to do or not to do. I was going to be in control of my *own* life and make my *own* decisions. I didn't care what the eventual consequences might be. I just lived each moment for the moment. It never occurred to me that by drinking so much at a young age I could end up being an alcoholic. It also never occurred to me that drinking could lead me to do some stupid and dangerous things. I was so rebellious that if I was told not to do something, I wanted to do it all the more. That attitude led to another stupid choice.

My mom had told me not to smoke. But at the age of eleven, I found some cigarettes lying on the ground and chose to pick them up. I took them home and hid them in my jewelry box. A few days later, a friend spent the night and we tried smoking them. Even though the taste was disgusting and it burned our throats, we tried it again and again until eventually it wasn't so bad. Those five cigarettes were gone pretty quick, but in those days (the eighties), they sold cigarettes in candy machines for only ninety cents. All we had to do was stand in front of the machine so no one could see what we were getting. We tried all the different brands and flavors and by the time we found one we liked, we were hooked. Once again, I didn't recognize the natural consequence of my rebellion. I just did whatever felt good.

Drinking and smoking felt good, but going to church didn't. In fact, it just made me angry. I was convinced that either God didn't exist or, if He did, He hated me. Either way, there was no way I was going to worship Him. So I refused to go to church.

The regular Sunday service I was able to get out of pretty easily, but Christmas Eve was a different story. It had been a family tradition for many years to go to the Candlelight Service at 11:00 PM and then come home and open one Christmas gift. Christmas was only about getting presents as far as I was concerned so, for a couple of years, I went to the service just to get the present. But then I decided that it wasn't worth it and I quit going altogether. I shut God completely out of my life until a friend invited me to spend the night with her on a Saturday night and go to her church with her and her mom on Sunday morning.

Back then I didn't know that much about the different denominations in the Christian faith. I just knew that my mom was raised Lutheran and my dad had been raised Catholic. I knew that Catholics are not allowed to marry outside of the Catholic faith, which meant that my dad had to choose between my mom and his religion. Obviously he chose her, or you wouldn't be reading this book right now.

Dad converted to Lutheran and my sisters and I were raised in a Lutheran church. But I decided that I didn't like the church. I didn't care for the "liturgy", although I didn't even know at the time what that was. All I knew was that I wasn't learning anything there and I usually came out with more questions than when I went in.

I'd gone to a few other churches from time to time with friends and family, but most of them seemed essentially the same to me. They all had boring sermons and music that made me yawn. I didn't pay all that much attention to the sermons because none of it mattered to me. It was all just a game as far as I was concerned. Different denominations just have different rules for how they play the game.

My husband and I enjoy playing pitch. That was one of the few things our parents had in common when we married. But they each had their own rules and preferences for how they played the card game. My husband's family played seventeen-point pitch, whereas my parents preferred ten-point. As we've played the game with other couples, we've found other differences. Some people pass the deck when they fill their hand while others continue to draw and "burn" any extra cards. Some players throw their cards in as soon as they play their last one in the bidding suit; others hold them until the next turn. Which of these rules is right? I don't know. For that matter, is it really important as long as everyone agrees on how to play?

It seems to me that that's how it is with religion. People decide how they want to "play the game". Each denomination makes up their own rules and calls it their "doctrine". It may or may not be Biblical, but it doesn't matter as long as everyone in the church agrees to it. If you don't like it, you can simply find another denomination. I didn't like how the Lutherans played the game, so I tried another denomination.

I talk a lot in this book about different religious denominations. I want to pause here to clarify that there is no one perfect denomination. If I refer to a church denomination in a negative way, please understand that I am basing my views and opinions on my experience of churches within that denomination. Your opinion and experience, of course, might be different.

Jeanne went to a Baptist church, which was a lot different than the Lutheran church I had attended. For one thing, it was a lot smaller and not nearly as fancy. Although some people were dressed in suits and dresses, others were wearing jeans and t-shirts. The pastor was wearing a suit and tie rather than a robe and white collar.

But the biggest difference that I noticed right away was the way they baptized. There was no small baptismal font in the front of the church like I had been used to. Jeanne explained that they didn't baptize babies in that church. Instead they baptized older children and adults after they accepted Christ.

Accepting Christ was a totally foreign concept to me. I had no idea what she was talking about, but I was intrigued and wanted to learn more. I not only attended that service, but I chose to come back again and even go to Sunday School.

Another difference that I found in the Baptist church was that the Bible was opened during every service—and not just by the pastor. The people in the congregation actually brought their own Bibles and read out of them! I had to find a Bible at home to bring so I wouldn't look out of place. I was able to find one, but I found it hard to follow along. My Bible was the King James Version and the pastor used the NIV (New International Version). But I found that it was OK, because instead of just reading a few selected verses to the congregation, the pastor actually talked about what they meant and even explained how we could apply them to our lives. I was finally beginning to get a taste of what was in this mysterious book.

I even began to read a little on my own. I really wanted to know what the Bible had to say about baptism. I found that it refers only to submersion in water after salvation and says nothing about baptizing babies. I later learned that baptism actually means, "to immerse or plunge". I decided that I wanted to keep going to the Baptist church. Their teachings seemed to be more Biblical, at least in regards to baptism. But more importantly, I *chose* that church, it wasn't chosen for me. I wanted to be in control of that too.

That summer, after I'd been attending church and Sunday School for a few months, I went to a youth rally with kids from other area churches. I'd never been to anything like that before. There was a Christian rock band playing. I didn't even know that Christian rock bands existed. Although the style of the music was a lot like what I was used to hearing on the radio, the lyrics had a very different message. I have to admit, though, that I wasn't really listening that closely because the lead singer was really good-looking and I couldn't take my eyes off of him. But as I stared at him, I noticed that it wasn't just his physical appearance that captured my attention. He had an appeal about him that went way beyond his looks or his musical talent. There was something else about him that I just couldn't identify.

As the music wound down, I saw something I had never seen before. The singer's attitude changed. He became more serious. He began talking about why the band performs at these youth rallies. He talked about their faith in Christ. I was in awe as I listened to him. He then made an invitation for anyone to step forward and profess their faith in Christ.

After a few moments of silence, I saw many kids stand up and make their way to the stage. I wanted what they had. I wanted the joy, excitement, and hope that I saw on their faces. I wanted something that might fill the emptiness.

Although I still didn't fully understand it all, I stood up and joined the crowd. I said that I wanted to accept Jesus Christ as my Savior.

The singer led the group through a prayer that we all repeated. After we said, "Amen," I looked around at all of the other kids. Some were cheering, some were weeping. Many were hugging one another. I didn't know any of them, so I just went back to my seat to watch the rest of the show. On the way home, I wondered if what I had just done would have any effect on me. If Jesus really had entered my heart, I expected my life to be suddenly transformed from that very moment. So I waited . . .

CHAPTER 3

The "game" of Christianity

When I got engaged to my husband, my family decided that we needed to teach him to play our favorite card game. If he was to be a member of our family, he had to learn to play "Shanghai".

Now Shanghai is a simple, yet complex, game. It's easy to play, if you know all the rules—and there are many. After inundating Robert with all of the ins and outs of this progressive card game for several minutes, we decided to play a hand and he could pick up the rest of the rules as we went along.

Everything seemed to be going along just fine until Robert broke a rule by laying down a run with mixed suits. Of course, he didn't know that he had broken a rule because it was one that we had forgotten to mention. It seemed obvious to us that a run must be all in one suit, but we had been playing the game for many years. It was not obvious to a new player.

That's how I felt like after the youth rally. I felt like a new player in the game of Christianity and the seasoned Christians failed to explain all of the rules to me. Maybe they expected me to just "pick it up". But what I picked up wasn't what I bargained for.

Soon after the rally, I began to recognize hypocrisy in the church. The kids in Sunday School, even those who had attended the youth rally, were just as sinful as the kids who didn't even go to church. They had all the Biblical head knowledge, but it didn't seem to have found its way into their hearts. They could be reciting Bible verses one minute and turn right around and insult their classmates the next. It seemed to me that you could temporarily drop out of the game of Christianity whenever you felt like it and drop back in when it was convenient.

Even worse, instead of mentoring me as a new Christian and helping me to grow in Christ, the pastor failed to demonstrate an example of Christlikeness. My friend's mother quit attending the church because the pastor told a divorced woman that she was no longer welcome. The "rule" of Christianity that I learned from him was that the standards of membership are really high – higher than I could possibly attain. Although I kept going, my heart was hardened to the message. It became meaningless. Jesus explains what happened to me in the parable of the four soils in Matthew 13, verses 18-21. I would be described as the rocky soil. I heard the message and received it with real joy, but I didn't have much depth, the seeds didn't take root. Soon trouble came and I dropped out.

I thought about my early experiences with hypocrisy when I was asked to give a children's sermon at church decades later. I knew how important it was for those kids to realize that, as Christians, we represent Christ in the way we live and treat others. If we are filled with the Holy Spirit, the Spirit should flow out of us. Sadly, I knew from experience that many times it is difficult to tell the difference between Christians and non-Christians, even in churches. I used Coke cans to illustrate this point.

I held up two cans and asked the kids, "Who can tell me what's in these cans?"

As expected, they all yelled, "Coke!"

I asked, "How do you know?"

"Because it says 'Coke' on the cans," they answered.

I explained that the cans represent two people who both claim to be Christians. On the outside, they look the same. "But how do we really know what's in these cans?"

One child gave the answer I was looking for. "You pour them out," she said.

"That's right, I said. "The only way to really know what's inside something, or someone, is to see what pours out. You see, some people say that they are Christians, but they lie, cheat, steal, or disobey their parents. What pours out of them is no different than what pours out of those who are not Christians."

I tipped the first can and poured Coke into a clear glass.

"But when the Holy Spirit comes into the life of a Christian, that person is changed on the inside. The outside might look the same, but what pours out is different."

I tipped the second can and poured clear water out as I explained, "What pours out of that person is pure and holy. We see evidence that the person is a Christian by what pours out of them."

After my "salvation", I saw no evidence of genuine Christianity around me. I am not saying that there were no genuine Christians in that church. I am sure there were, but I wasn't noticing them. The hypocrites stood out far more. As a result, I became bitter toward Christianity. It wasn't what I thought it was and I decided that I didn't want any part of it. Instead I found myself drawn to something else.

Although I continued to go to church, I lived a double life. While in church, I played the game. But once I walked out the door, I stepped into darkness. I became interested in books and movies about the supernatural. I read everything I could get my hands on about ghosts, ESP, psychic powers, and the occult. I loved horror movies and horror novels. I had no idea how they were affecting me. I now know that messed up people mess up other people. What I was letting into my head messed me up.

Many times during my childhood, I had sung, "Oh be careful little eyes what you see", but I didn't heed the warning. I let anything and everything in. Proverbs 15:14 says, "A wise person is hungry for knowledge, while the fool feeds on trash." (NLT) I was feeding on a whole lot of trash and was making some pretty bad choices as a result of my poor media "diet".

I began to believe that maybe Satan could give me what God hadn't. Maybe "the dark side" could give me that sense of power and control that I so desperately craved. To access that power, I decided to start a "satanic cult". Some kids that I knew had a Ouija board. We would have slumber parties and use the board to call upon evil spirits to foretell the future or gain information that would otherwise be unknown to us. We would even do séances in an attempt to communicate with spirits. We had no idea what we were doing or what demonic forces we were opening ourselves up to. We were just doing what we'd seen on TV and in movies.

I had left God's hand, which we are all free to do at any time. As you see on the cover of this book, God's hand is open. He reaches out and waits for us to place ourselves in His hand. Once we do, He doesn't hold us in a closed fist. We're free to leave His control at any time. And that was what I did. I left His control and His protection. But I didn't just open myself up to being grabbed by Satan; I chose to purposely place myself in his hand. I was playing a new and dangerous game and I didn't know the rules to this one either.

Thankfully it didn't take long for me to discover that things are not the same in real life as they are in the movies. Satan worship didn't provide me with that sense of power and control that I was seeking. I didn't miraculously receive supernatural powers to wreak havoc on kids who bullied me or suddenly become popular. I still felt alone and empty. I gave up on outright worshipping Satan, but I continued to live my life in a way that pleased him, which was essentially the same thing.

I became even more rebellious. I shoplifted, vandalized, and even fraudulently used someone else's credit card. I refused to obey my parents at all. I would sneak out of the house in the middle of the night to hang out with my friends and tried running away from home several times to gain "freedom". Then that freedom was taken from me when I was locked up for three and a half days after running away.

I hated being a prisoner in that little concrete room. All I had ever wanted was freedom. I believed that experiencing "freedom" would bring me happiness. But instead I found that I was anything *but* happy.

Even when I was running, I wasn't happy. I was still miserable and as empty as ever.

I wrote a long letter to the judge asking him to let me go home. I said that I was ready to change and I really thought that I was. But I wasn't. I had the desire to change, but I didn't have the ability. I was powerless.

John 15:5 says, "I am the Vine, you are the branches. He who remains in Me, and I in him, bears much fruit. Apart from Me you can do nothing." (NIV) I hadn't remained in Him, so I could do nothing.

CHAPTER 4

A not so wonderful life

One of my favorite movies is, "It's a Wonderful Life". I watched it for the first time when I was a kid. But the movie didn't lead me to realize how great my life was. Instead, it just made me wish, like the character of George Bailey early in the movie, that I had never been born.

My life was not a wonderful life. No, it pretty much sucked. I couldn't see anything good about it for me, or anyone around me for that matter. By the end of the movie, George Bailey was able to see how his life had impacted others in amazingly positive ways. But I could see nothing positive in my life. I hadn't done anything good for anybody. I had done nothing but cause problems for the people around me. I believed that my life was worthless.

I wanted to die. I often thought about suicide as a way to end the constant pain of living my life. Drinking only lessened the pain and it always came back—oftentimes worse. I wanted the pain to end for good.

I began hoarding pills and hiding razor blades in preparation for ending my life. Much of my time was consumed with planning for my own demise. I was hospitalized a couple of times for suicide attempts, but was never in any real danger. I couldn't bring myself to make a genuine attempt because I was afraid of where I might go if I succeeded.

I wasn't entirely sure about the existence of Heaven and Hell. I knew that I didn't deserve to go to Heaven if it existed. And, if there was a hell, I knew I didn't want to go there. Yet I also didn't want to go on living my life feeling so empty and alone. I had to find some way to fill that ever-present void. Once again the media steered me really wrong.

What I saw in movies and on TV, what I read in teen romance novels, and what I heard in the lyrics of popular music led me to believe that having a boyfriend would bring me the happiness and fulfillment I had been so desperately seeking. Being in a relationship would "complete me". So I started "dating".

Now when you're a young teenager, there's really no such thing as "dating", which is why I put the word in quotations. You just say that you're going out with someone. So that was what I did. I said I was going out with a boy when I was thirteen. When that "relationship" ended, I started "dating" someone else and then someone else. But none of them brought me the fulfillment I was looking for.

As I was searching for "Mr. Right", I was also drinking—a lot. Drinking numbed my emotional pain and made me feel accepted. When I drank, I felt happy and could have fun. I began going to parties where I knew there would be drinking and I was drunk nearly every weekend.

I began drinking even more after I was introduced to wine coolers. Those actually did taste an awful lot like Kool-Aid. I could drink them easily and get drunk pretty quickly. I had started drinking to control my pain, but it wasn't long before alcohol began to control me. Instead of *wanting* to drink, I began to feel like I *needed* to drink. And when I drank, I *had* to get drunk. Once I was drunk, I lost complete control. Many times I drank to the point of vomiting or passing out. I put myself in some really bad situations, but refused to take responsibility for any of it.

I wouldn't have admitted it at the time, but I wanted to get drunk because I believed that then I wouldn't be responsible for my actions. I could do whatever I wanted when I was drunk and use the excuse that I didn't know what I was doing. It was like a free pass to be as reckless as

I wanted to be. But there was nothing free about my reckless behavior. I paid a price.

There were a lot of guys at those drinking parties and, because I had developed early, many of them were noticing me. I loved feeling desired and I was willing to compromise my "morals" to have that attention. But once I took that first step, I found that it was a slippery slope. After that first kiss, it was easy to go further with the next guy. Before I knew it, I was allowing guys to touch me in places that only my future husband should be touching. The next thing I knew, I was giving that precious gift of my virginity to someone I barely knew. I was only fifteen.

Whether or not I chose to accept responsibility for that decision didn't matter. The result was the same. I was no longer a virgin. And once your virginity is gone, you can't get it back again, although I desperately wished that I could have.

That experience should have been shared with the person I would spend the rest of my life with. Instead it was shared with someone I never wanted to see again. I did become quite popular with other guys. But, of course, they only wanted to date me for one reason. My next relationship after that was purely sexual and lasted only a couple of months, but there was another guy that was interested—a much older guy.

At sixteen, I began dating a 21-year-old. I thought it was pretty cool to have a grown man interested in me and I didn't see a problem with dating him. But there was a problem—a big problem. The only reason a 21-year-old man would want to date a 16-year-old girl is for sex. It was a price I was willing to pay to feel loved. But that "loving feeling" didn't last. I began feeling cheap and used. I told him that the relationship wasn't working and that I wanted to break up. He wasn't willing to let go that easily. He threw me down on his bed and raped me.

I tried to fight, but went completely limp when he said, "The more you fight, the more turned on I get." I couldn't believe that I had trusted this man. I had allowed myself to trust and therefore allowed myself to get hurt—really hurt.

When it was over, I couldn't move for several minutes. I felt so scared and alone. I didn't know what to do. Finally I decided that I would make him pay for what he had done to me. I left the apartment and drove straight to the police station.

I had to go to the hospital for a rape exam, which was like being raped all over again. It was humiliating and painful. They had to keep my clothes for evidence, so I had to call home to have someone bring me other clothes. I did not want to make that call. Mom had told me not to date this guy and I had to admit that she was right. I was grateful when she said that she would send Dad with the clothes.

But when Dad arrived, he wasn't alone. He brought someone from Campus Life. I'd gone to a few of their meetings when I was still going to church. I quit going because many of the kids there were hypocrites also. I didn't get to know the leaders very well and didn't even recognize this man standing next to my father. I really didn't understand why Dad had even brought him. But when he offered me a guestroom to sleep in for the night, I was grateful and accepted the offer.

I don't even remember the drive to the family's home. I don't think I talked at all and I went straight to bed when we arrived. I didn't want to give that man a chance to start preaching to me or trying to tell me that God loves me because I would *not* believe that. I believed that God hated me. Why else would He have allowed something like that to happen to me?

I decided that I wanted nothing to do with God after that. Although He had clearly reached out to me through that man, I refused to see it. I wouldn't even acknowledge Him. I had my back turned on God, making it impossible for me to see Him even if I wanted to, which I didn't.

I pulled further and further away from God as I went my own way. C.S. Lewis once said, "There are two kinds of people: those who say to God, 'Thy will be done,' and those to whom God says, 'All right, then, have it your way.'" I wanted to have it my way and God let me.

But I didn't know where "my way" would lead. I was wandering around aimlessly in the dark, trying to find anything or anyone to fill that emptiness in my heart. I continued to drink and continued to get involved in more and more bad relationships. It was a pattern I just couldn't break. My desire for "freedom" from God's rules was leading me into an inescapable bondage to sin.

I couldn't see the potential consequences of my ongoing immoral behavior and wouldn't even acknowledge it when others did. When I was about sixteen or seventeen, one of my sister's college roommates told me, "If you keep this up, you're gonna be pregnant by eighteen." I didn't listen to her, but I should have because her words proved to be prophetic. At eighteen, I found myself pregnant.

I shouldn't have been surprised. I didn't always practice "safe sex". But even if I had, it might not have mattered because there's no such thing as "safe sex", which is why I put it in quotation marks. We all know that pregnancies occur in spite of contraceptive measures and that STDs are transmitted even when condoms are used. But beyond the physical consequences, the "safe sex" that is taught in public schools and talked about in the media does not take into account the devastating emotional effects that sex outside of marriage brings. No one had taught me any of what I really needed to know about sex. I was trying to figure it out on my own and therefore was experiencing a lot of negative consequences as a result of my ignorance of God's perfect plan.

I already felt like garbage from being used and thrown away by guys. But now I had to face something on my own that should only be experienced by a married couple. What should be a joyous event to be shared with family and friends was devastating to me and I was afraid to tell anyone about it.

CHAPTER 5

The right to "choose"

I felt so alone as I stared at those two lines on the pregnancy test. I didn't know what I was going to do. All of the "options" came to mind and I contemplated each of them. A few months earlier I had registered to vote for the first time. I registered as a Democrat because I believed in a woman's right to "choose". But now I was facing that very choice myself—and that made it a lot different.

Although I believed that a pregnancy was only a "potential life," somehow I immediately felt a connection to that little life inside of me. I knew in my heart that it would be wrong to end that life. So I considered having the baby and trying to be a parent at eighteen. It didn't take long for me to decide to cross that option off the list. I knew that I was not ready to be a mother. I couldn't even take care of myself. How could I take care of a baby?

Next, I considered adoption. It really seemed like the best choice. My baby would live and be cared for by a husband and wife who were ready to be parents. It was the most loving and selfless choice I could make. I made some calls to adoption agencies and found out that the father and I could even choose the couple that we wanted to care for our baby. He was in agreement and we both felt good about what we had decided. But others didn't feel so good about it.

When I told my parents about the pregnancy and my decision, my mom expressed concern that I wouldn't be able to give up the baby once it was born. My friends thought that it was wrong for me to consider "giving away" my baby. Then the father began to question whether the baby was even his and he left me. I felt no support in my decision. I was completely alone.

That was when doubt began to creep in. I thought about how tough it would be being pregnant in college. I knew that I would have to make serious changes to my lifestyle and I wasn't sure that I was willing to make those changes. The pendulum swung the other direction. Instead of considering what was best for my baby, I began thinking only about myself. That other "option" returned to the list.

I continued to feel a connection to the tiny person growing inside me. The longer I stayed pregnant, the stronger that connection grew. I even made a promise to that little life that I would protect it—but it was a promise that I would fail to keep.

After the father and I broke up, I met a new guy that I really liked. I thought that he might be "the one". I was sure that he wouldn't want to be with me if he knew that I was pregnant, so I didn't tell him. Instead, I called an abortion clinic.

I was told that since I was still in my first trimester, it would be a simple "procedure". They could even put me under general anesthesia if I wanted. I would be completely asleep and feel absolutely nothing. That sounded good to me, so I made the appointment.

My mother went with me. When we arrived at the clinic and prepared to get out of the car, we found ourselves surrounded by protestors. I vividly recall one of them coming up to us and addressing my mother directly. She said, "If you love her, you won't let her do this." The clinic staff came to our "rescue" and escorted us into the facility, but those words kept replaying in my mind. I thought to myself, "She does love me and that is why she is letting me do this," and yet I began to wonder.

I didn't wonder whether or not my mother loved me. I knew she did and I knew that she believed that I was doing the right thing. I think most parents whose daughters abort think that they are doing the right thing. But once we were inside the clinic, I started to become apprehensive. *I* wasn't sure I was doing the right thing.

I asked if I could see a counselor, but was informed that there wasn't one available. If I really wanted to see one, we would have to reschedule. We were four hours from home. I knew that it wasn't practical to make another eight-hour trip, so I signed the consent form.

What I didn't know then is that abortion is a multi-million dollar industry. Abortionists are not in business to help women; they are in business to make money. Pro-choice is really pro-abortion. They want women who find themselves facing an unplanned pregnancy to "choose" to abort. That's how they stay in business. If they had offered me a counselor, I might have changed my mind and left, taking my money with me. But any "counseling" they might have offered probably would have counseled me to abort. Either way, they had me once they got me in the door.

After the paperwork was complete, they led me to an examination room to undergo a pre-surgical exam. It reminded me a lot of the rape exam and I just wanted it to be over quickly. The doctor said, "It looks like you're about nine weeks pregnant." That meant nothing to me. As far as I knew, I was just carrying a blob of tissue, only a "potential life". That's what I had called it when I did a persuasive speech in high school: a "potential life". I had to believe that, because if what I was carrying in my womb was already a life, then I was about to commit murder.

I shut off the connection that I felt. I closed my eyes and waited to go to sleep, looking forward to waking up with the "problem" gone.

When I awakened, I felt some physical pain and asked them to give me something for it. All they offered me was Advil. I really wanted some strong narcotic—anything to keep me from thinking. For a long time after that, I did everything I could to keep from thinking about it. I drank even more, took narcotic pain meds whenever I could get my hands on them, and slept as much I could.

I had started dating the guy that I aborted for and I told him about what I had done. He said that he would have still dated me, but he supported my decision. He tried to protect me from pro-life "propaganda" by changing the channel when pro-life messages aired on television during election times.

Then, two years later, I saw a pregnancy brochure in a doctor's office. I don't know why, but I picked it up and opened it. Inside I saw pictures of fetuses at different gestational ages. As I looked at the windows into the womb, I couldn't believe what I was seeing. The caption under the photo at five weeks said, "At this stage, the fetus has a beating heart." One image showed a fetus at nine weeks gestational age, the same age as the one I had aborted. But I didn't see a blob of tissue in that picture. I saw a tiny human being with arms and legs, eyes and ears. This wasn't a "potential" life; it was a *real* life! I suddenly realized what I had done. I had killed a baby!

I left the office and ran out to my car where I broke down bawling. *If only I could go back and change that decision. If only I would have kept my promise. If only I had chosen to give my baby life.*

But there was no going back. It was too late. That life was ended and it was my fault. The guilt I felt was unbearable. I was sure that if there was a God, there was no way He could forgive me for this. I believed that some sins were worse than others and that murder was the worst. So murder of the most vulnerable had to be the absolute worst.

I had to fix it. I had to do something to make it right. In my finite, human mind I thought that there was a way for me to atone for my sin and correct the mistake. I decided that I would replace the baby I had killed. Maybe then God could forgive me.

My current boyfriend was not interested in helping me, so I seduced a co-worker and got pregnant. I vowed to do the right thing this time. As soon as I saw the positive sign on the pregnancy test, I called an adoption agency and told them of my intent to place my baby for adoption. I felt some relief and was certain that this would make everything better. But only a few weeks later, I began bleeding. An ultrasound confirmed that I had miscarried.

I was devastated. Not only did the abortion clinic staff not tell me that my baby had a beating heart, but they also did not tell me that subsequent pregnancies after abortion often end in miscarriage. I believed that God was punishing me for what I had done. I believed that I had committed an unforgivable sin. I had taken a life and I believed that I deserved to die for it.

Suicide was all I could think about, yet I was afraid. Someone told me that everyone who commits suicide goes to Hell and I believed that. That belief often kept me from following through. But someone else kept me from taking my life many times and I don't think he even knew it.

CHAPTER 6

These guys are different

Jeff was one of my best friends in college. He was different than most of the guys I hung around. He didn't go to parties and, as far as I knew, he didn't even drink. Instead, he spent most of his time in campus ministry activities or at church. I thought that was pretty weird and I really didn't understand why he would want to be my friend. We had very little in common, yet somehow I enjoyed hanging out with him.

What intrigued me the most was that, despite my immoral activities, Jeff didn't judge me. He also didn't join me. I had another friend who claimed to be a Christian, but she went to the bars, got drunk quite often, and had a lot of boyfriends. She talked the talk well, but she didn't walk the walk. Jeff, on the other hand, walked the walk. He was a different kind of Christian than any I had previously met. He seemed genuine, like the real thing.

Jeff knew that I was confused about faith and invited me to his church. It was Pentecostal and I had been to that kind of church once with my sister. The people were babbling in some weird language and waving their arms and crying. All I wanted to do was get out of there. The campus church Jeff was involved with was Lutheran and I didn't want to try that again either. Jeff told me to choose any church and he would go with me. I liked the beliefs of the Baptist church so we went to a few Baptist churches together.

Every week I was absolutely amazed that the sermons seemed to speak directly to me. It was almost eerie how the pastors seemed to know just what I needed to hear. It made me a little uncomfortable and many times I wanted to run out. But I was too scared. The last thing I wanted to do in church was to call attention to myself. So I stayed and I tried to listen, but the message just wasn't sinking in. The guilt I carried over the abortion kept getting in the way.

I truly believed that God could never love or accept me again. I became more depressed and more suicidal. The fear of Hell was no longer a concern. I believed that I was going there anyway. Suicide was just speeding up the inevitable.

I came very close to ending my life many times. But besides being weird in almost every way, Jeff also seemed to have this innate ability to know when I was at my lowest points. Countless times when I was about to swallow a bottle of pills or slit my wrist with a razor blade, Jeff would just happen to call or stop by. It was like he somehow knew that I needed him, although there was no way that he could; at least no way that I knew of.

I don't think Jeff ever knew how many times he saved my life. He just knew that I needed God and he was desperately trying to show Him to me. He knew how lost I was and that I needed a guide, a map, and a flashlight to find my way.

When our two sons were seven and nine, my husband and I took them through an exercise to illustrate their need for guidance. We had Randal and Justin list all of the possible pitfalls they could encounter on their journey through adolescence as I wrote each one on separate sheets of paper. I then scattered the papers all over the floor of our basement. We turned off all of the lights and it was pitch dark.

Randal, as the oldest, went first. He was instructed to walk through the family room and up the stairs, picking up any paper that he stepped on, symbolizing falling into that pitfall. Justin then followed him, picking up any papers that he stepped on along his way. When they were done, we looked at all of the pitfalls they had fallen into because they could not see them.

Naturally Randal fell into the most because there were more there. Justin had fewer because he didn't fall into the same ones that his brother had. In real life, he would hopefully learn from his brother's mistakes and not make the same ones.

This exercise allowed the boys to see just how easy it is to fall into the traps of alcoholism, teenage fatherhood, or gang involvement without having to actually experience any of these trials firsthand. We then asked the boys if it would have been easier going through this exercise with a map of the pitfalls and how to go around them, or a flashlight illuminating what was right in front of them, or a personal guide who had been down the path already. Of course they said that any one of those would have made the walk much easier.

We explained to our sons that they have all three of these on their real-life journey. God provides us a roadmap in the Bible. He tells us about all of the pitfalls and how to avoid them. Psalms 119:19 says, "I am but a pilgrim here on earth: how I need a map—and Your commands are my chart and guide."

God also gives us the Holy Spirit to be our flashlight. The Spirit lets us know when we are about to do something that we shouldn't and helps us get back on the right path. In addition, God provides us with guides, those who have been through the journey and know where those pitfalls are, either because they managed to avoid them or because they fell into them. Randal and Justin were given each type of guide. Their father had avoided most of the pitfalls on his journey while I had fallen into most of them.

Jeff gave me a Bible while we were in college together, but I didn't see it as a roadmap. Instead I saw it as rulebook and therefore refused to open it. I believed that it would just confirm what a rotten sinner I was and tell me that I could never live up to God's standards. I had no idea that reading that book could free me from my sin and give me the hope that I could not find anywhere else. Psalms 119:31 says, "I cling to Your commands and follow them as closely as I can. Lord, don't let me make a mess of things." I didn't read that. I didn't follow His commands, so I made a mess of things.

After Jeff moved away, I quit going to church. I continued to believe that God could never forgive me for all of my mistakes, so there was no point in trying to seek His forgiveness. It was much easier to just go right on sinning. So that's what I did.

I had finally turned twenty-one and began going to the bars every weekend. I met a lot of guys and again began getting involved in relationships to find fulfillment. But none of them provided me fulfillment. Instead they left me feeling empty and used—until I met Robert.

Robert was also in college and lived across the alley from me. He would come over nearly every day to just talk. He seemed genuinely interested in getting to know me and, like Jeff, didn't judge me when he learned what kind of person I was.

Robert didn't go to church and didn't talk "Christian". I didn't even know if he was a Christian for some time. I just knew that there was something different about him. He didn't smoke and didn't drink at all. I had recently decided to quit smoking and hanging out with Robert was actually more enjoyable than going to the bars, so I cut way back on drinking too.

Our friendship grew and eventually Robert asked me out on a date. It was strange and kind of refreshing dating a friend. I'd never done that before. Of course, the dynamics of our relationship changed once we started dating. I assumed that, like my other relationships, it would become sexual right away. But instead, Robert said something that caused me to fall in love with him. He said, "I care about you too much to have sex with you."

I knew right then and there that I wanted to spend the rest of my life with this man. Two months later Robert proposed and I accepted. We were engaged two days before my college graduation.

I wish I could say that we waited until our wedding night to have sex, but we didn't. Robert was (and still is) a Christian, but not long before he met me, he had stumbled. He chose to do something that he had said he would never do.

Believing that he would never get married, at the age of twenty, Robert chose to give up his virginity just to experience sex. He regretted that decision as much as I regretted my choice to give away my virginity years earlier. Since neither of us were virgins, waiting until after the wedding didn't seem so important. I certainly didn't see a problem with it. Sex wasn't a big deal to me.

I have to admit that of all of the bad choices that I made after choosing to turn my back on God, dating and becoming sexually active as a teenager were the worst. Had I remained a virgin and experienced sex only with my husband, I never would have experienced the rape, I never would have gotten pregnant out of wedlock, and I never would have had an abortion and subsequent miscarriage.

I now realize that most of the pain that I suffered in my life was self-inflicted. I brought on my own problems by trying to do things my own way. Had I listened to the Creator of life, I would never have created the mess that I did in my life.

Thankfully, Randal learned much earlier than I did. Although he chose to try out the "dating" thing in middle school, he then read *I Kissed Dating Goodbye* by Joshua Harris. In that book, he learned that dating is preparation for marriage. If you're not ready to get married, you shouldn't date. Randal was not ready to get married at fourteen and therefore decided to forego dating altogether until college.

Justin learned from Randal's mistake and made the same choice—before dating at all. He won't even hug a girl. From watching and listening to her brothers, and her parents, Sheila has chosen to have her first kiss at her wedding.

I am so grateful to see my kids making good choices that will spare them the pain I have suffered. There is no guarantee that they will stick to them, but with their desire to remain pure and the power of the Holy Spirit in their lives, not to mention very supportive parents, I think they will succeed. If they do, they and their future spouses will be blessed with far greater intimacy in their marriage then Robert and I would achieve.

Because Robert and I had both chosen to break the seventh commandment and had sex with people who were not our spouses, our first time together was not our first time. It was tainted and not the pure and holy experience that it was meant to be. Even if we had both been virgins at the time, we would have still corrupted the experience by having sex with each other before our wedding night.

If you are unmarried and you are a virgin, I pray that you will stay that way until you marry. You will be giving your spouse a precious and priceless gift. If you're already having sex and you're not married, I implore you to stop. Although damage has already been done, you can minimize it by stopping now. And you may save yourself from making other unwise choices, because once you take that first step toward sexual immorality, it's a slippery slope.

Because having sex prior to marriage wasn't a big deal, living together before marriage wasn't a big deal either. Robert and I both needed to move out of our apartments, so we lived together for our yearlong engagement for "convenience". But convenience comes at a price.

Living together was like making a commitment without really making a commitment. I knew that I could break off the engagement, but it would be harder than if we were living apart. I began to feel trapped even before we were married.

A couple's engagement period is to be a time of excitement and anticipation. We never had that. There was no anticipation. We were already living as a married couple. We had nothing new to look forward to after the wedding. The only thing that would change would be my last name.

Not only did I not have much to look forward to after the wedding, I wasn't even looking forward to the wedding itself. I learned that Robert's family had a tradition of stealing the bride after weddings and taking her out to get her drunk. I did not want any part of that tradition.

I made it clear to Robert that I would not be *stolen* and he agreed to share my wishes with his family. I felt confident when we arrived at the dance that his family was respecting my wishes. But shortly after arriving, Robert disappeared. I never guessed that they might steal him. I had no idea where he was or when he might return. While he was gone, some other family members tried to steal me and he wasn't there to protect me. I had to fight them off on my own.

I felt utterly betrayed. This man who had just pledged to love and honor me till death abandoned me within hours of his vow. During the forty-five minutes that Robert was gone, I felt tremendous regret and wished that I hadn't married him. I strongly considered throwing away the unsigned marriage license and just calling it quits. But we were already living together. How could I get out? It was too late. I was stuck.

CHAPTER 7

Seeing His hand

Although I felt stuck in my marriage, I really wasn't and *that* was the problem. Many years later, I heard a woman speaking on abstinence at my son's school. What she said made a lot of sense to me and I wished that I had heard it decades earlier. She explained that when we're virgins, we're like a new strip of adhesive tape that easily bonds. When we have sex, we bond ourselves to another person. She illustrated this by putting packing tape on a person's arm. She said that when we break up with that person, we take some of them with us. She peeled off the tape and showed the skin and hair that came off with it. When we "hook up" with someone else, we take some of that person also. Each relationship that ends, leaves us with more and more residue until eventually we're no longer sticky. By the time we marry, we're unable to bond.

I wasn't sticky anymore. I had been in so many relationships before I met Robert, that I was covered in residue. I couldn't bond to my husband. Although we managed to stay together, it was not a real marriage. Instead, we were like roommates who shared a bed and a last name.

We faced other major stressors right from the beginning that didn't help. A year before we married, I was diagnosed with endometriosis, which is a disease that causes endometrial tissue, or uterine lining, to be found outside of the uterus. The disease caused such intense pain that I wanted to die. I believed it was just another sign that God hated me and was punishing me for living my life in such an unholy way.

Doctors told us that pregnancy could put the disease in remission, but Robert and I weren't sure that we wanted to be parents. Then Robert's grandmother had a stroke. While visiting her in the hospital, we looked at all of her family gathered around her bed. We decided that we wanted that too. We wanted a family.

But we knew that it wouldn't be easy. I had already had one ovary removed due to the endometriosis. I also knew that my previous abortion could still lessen my chances of conceiving or maintaining a pregnancy. As I considered the possibility that I might not ever have a child because of that choice, I regretted it all the more. I wished that I would have known then what I know now. Life, *all* life, is a gift from God and we do not have the right to take life from anyone, born or unborn. Only God is the giver and taker of life.

Although I denied God at that time, I had to count on Him to give me a baby. So just in case He was there and listening, I prayed to Him to give us a child—and He answered. The second month after we began trying, I conceived. Thirty-six weeks later, I gave birth to my first child.

Because he was four weeks early, Randal had some breathing difficulties. They took him to the nursery to monitor him more closely and it was nearly four hours before I was able to hold him. Finally, the nurse brought him to me and placed my baby in my arms. I looked at this tiny person all wrapped up like a little burrito and something in my heart moved.

I studied Randal's face and his tiny eyelashes. I unwrapped him and looked at his little fingers and toes. I caressed the hair on his perfectly shaped head and touched his soft lips. Suddenly all doubt about whether or not God exists completely vanished. I knew that something like this does not happen by accident. Something this amazing does not "evolve" from nothing. This was proof of creation and proof of a divine Creator. I was convinced. I acknowledged at that moment that there truly is a God and that, despite all of my mistakes, He had chosen to bless me with this beautiful child.

After Randal's birth, I looked back over my life and recognized how God had been reaching out to me all along. I finally saw His hand. He had taken care of me after the rape through that person from Campus Life. He was the One who told Jeff to call or come over every time I was ready to end life. And He had tried to lead me away from having the abortion by letting me feel that connection to the baby.

I knew then that God was real. I *believed* in Him. But like when I supposedly accepted Christ as a teenager, nothing felt any different. I thought that believing in God made me a "Christian", but I had simply come to acknowledge His existence. Believing in Him didn't take away my past sins or relieve me of the guilt that I felt. I had recognized His hand, but I had not placed myself in it. If anything, acknowledging God's existence only made me feel more guilt. I still believed that I could never live up to His standards.

While I was pregnant with Randal, we had started going to church. It just seemed like the right thing to do when we were starting a family. But after Randal was born, we changed churches because there weren't any other young families there. I was glad we made the change, because at the new church, I began to understand a little more about Christianity.

I learned that Christianity is not a game or a way of life. It's a new life. Salvation doesn't mean following a set of rules or changing the way you act. It means being freed from sin and having new desires. 2 Corinthians 5:17 says, "When someone becomes a Christian he becomes a brand new person inside. He is not the same any more. A new life has begun!"

The new life that God had given me in Randal led me to want to become a Christian and begin a new life in myself. I wanted God's forgiveness. I didn't want to have to hold on to the guilt any more. I wanted to give it all over to Him. I longed to be in God's presence, but remembrances of my sins kept me away.

While writing this book, my pastor at the time gave a word picture that illustrated this so well. Pastor Charlie explained that when our sins are washed clean by the blood of Jesus it's like standing under a waterfall and having someone throw mud at you. It just won't stick. My problem was that I hadn't stepped into the waterfall, so everything Satan threw at me stuck.

Each time I came close to making a decision for Christ, I felt guilt. I was reminded of what a rotten sinner I was. I believed that I didn't deserve forgiveness. Since that time, I've come to learn that God never reminds us of our sins. He forgives and forgets. Hebrews 10:17 says, "I will never again remember their sins and lawless deeds." Satan, however, reminds us of our sin every chance he gets. As I sought to know God and came closer to choosing His hand, Satan attacked harder. He continued to remind me of my sins and even made me question what I was learning about God's standards.

I was in graduate school when Randal was born and, while studying to be a counselor, I was bombarded with liberal messages. In my Multicultural Counseling class, I was taught that homosexuals are another "culture" to be accepted and respected as much as any other culture. I really struggled with that. I learned in church and through my Bible reading that homosexual acts are sinful, even called an "abomination" in Leviticus 18:22. But my professor told me that homosexuals would likely make up ten percent of my caseload, so I would have to learn how to work with them.

A project for the class was to immerse myself in another culture. I chose to go to a homosexual church. That seemed to be the best way to address the Biblical issues. It was a good choice because an amazing thing happened to me at that church. It was the first time that I felt God "speak" to me.

As I looked around at all of the people in that sanctuary, I heard God telling me in my mind, "Love these sinners just as I love you. But do not condone their sin anymore than I condone yours."

I knew that God loved those people in that church and I knew that He loved me. But I didn't think He could accept me. Because God doesn't condone sin, I believed that I had to do something to get rid of my past sins and to stop sinning before I could become a Christian. That was really hard. No, actually, it was impossible. There was no way I could make up for the sins I'd already committed and, no matter how hard I tried, I couldn't stop sinning altogether. It seemed hopeless. I was ready to just give up, until I saw something that gave me some hope.

In the Baptist church, I saw people being baptized. I heard their testimonies of salvation. Some of them had lived very sinful lives and had chosen to accept God's forgiveness and turn away from their sin. The Holy Spirit could then begin to transform them to be more like Christ. Each one of them was beginning that new life that I wanted.

But each time I thought about "new life", I thought about the new life that I had ended with the abortion. Satan continued to remind me of *that* sin and convinced me that God could never forgive me for it. I might have learned differently if I had told someone in the church about it, but I was too afraid. Even if I wanted to, I wouldn't have the chance, because we had to leave.

Robert's first teaching job out of college ended due to budget cuts. We had to leave Kearney and move to Grand Island where he found a new job. That meant finding a new church, which was harder than we thought it might be.

We tried several Baptist churches, but none really fit for us. Most had no other young families. One church had to open the nursery just for us. Some of Robert's students attended the Evangelical Free Church, so we decided to give it a try, not really knowing what "Evangelical Free" meant.

As soon as we walked in the door, we felt at home. We loved the contemporary style of music and the uplifting atmosphere. There were plenty of young families there and many opportunities for us to get involved in small groups. And they had a great nursery, already open and filled with children.

But before we could commit to this church, Robert wanted to be certain that their beliefs were completely Biblical. I learned that the church doctrine is far more important than the denomination. We had the pastor come over and questioned him on the church's beliefs. We were pleased to find that it all fit with what Robert knew to be true from the Bible, so we made the E-Free Church our church home.

CHAPTER 8

The right choice

Soon after we started attending the E-Free church, I got into a young mom's Bible study since I was pregnant with our second son. I made some good friends and learned a lot through that Bible study. And I learned even more through the sermons every Sunday. I finally began to really understand the meaning of the most quoted verse of the Bible—John 3:16.

For God so loved the world that He gave His one and only Son, that whosoever believes in Him shall not perish but have eternal life. (NIV)

One of my reasons for denying God's existence was that I struggled with believing in a God who would "send" people to Hell. I think a lot of people have that same issue. God doesn't seem so loving and merciful when you hear, "believe or perish". I didn't want to believe in a God who would *force* me to believe in Him.

It all began to make sense when one of the pastors at E-Free compared the offer of salvation to being offered a free ticket to a concert or a sporting event. We can accept it or refuse it. When the event happens, those who refused the ticket will see what they're missing and many will try to get in, but they won't be admitted because they don't have a ticket. The pastor asked, "Can you really blame the One who offered the ticket when you regret your choice?" Of course not. We have only ourselves to blame.

That's how it is with God's offer of salvation. He doesn't *send* anyone to Hell; He wants to save us from it. He offers all of us a free ticket to Heaven. We don't deserve it, but He offers it to us anyway. There's nothing we can do to *earn* it. All we have to do is *accept* it.

I also learned that God does not qualify sin. Only we do that. In God's eyes, sin is sin. Lying is the same as murder. Taking God's name in vain is the same as adultery. And any sin, no matter how big or small in our minds, will separate us from Him. We all deserve to go to Hell because we all have sinned. Romans 3:23 says that "all have sinned and fall short of the glory of God." (NIV)

The first half of Romans 6:23 says that the wages of sin is death. Here it is talking about the second death. We will all die a physical death unless we are still here when Jesus returns. The second death means eternal separation from God, otherwise known as Hell. God is just and He must punish sin, but God is also loving and merciful. He loves us so much that He provided a way back to Him. He gave us a way to have eternal *life*, otherwise known as Heaven.

The free gift offered to us came at a price, but it's a price we don't have to pay because Jesus paid it for us. We deserve death for our sins, but Jesus came into this world to suffer and die for us that we may have life. He took the penalty for our sin so that we don't have to. The pastor described it like this: "He paid a debt He didn't owe because we owed a debt we couldn't pay."

The second half of Romans 6:23 says that the free gift of God is eternal life through Christ our Lord. Jesus is the only One who has ever lived a sinless life. He became the perfect sacrifice once and for all. Before He came, animals were sacrificed to atone for sin. But that sacrifice had to be made over and over again. When Jesus went to the cross, He gave His life to atone for *all* sin. No further sacrifice would have to be made. When He said, "It is finished," He meant it.

I finally realized that God didn't want to punish me; He wanted to save me. He didn't hate me; He loved me. I also realized that nothing I could do could ever make me right with God. Replacing that baby couldn't take away the sin of the abortion. Going to church or doing good works couldn't make me holy. Only through the sacrifice of Jesus, the Lamb of God, could I be made righteous. There was no other way. Jesus said, "I am the Way and the Truth and the Life, no one comes to the Father but through Me." (John 14:6) There is only one answer, only one way to salvation, and that way is Jesus.

I finally understood who Jesus is and what He did for me. He paid for my sins—*all* of my sins. 1 John 1:9 says, "If we confess our sins, He is faithful and just and will forgive us our sins and purify us from all unrighteousness." (NIV) The only unforgivable sin is denying Christ. Once we accept Him, all of our sins are forgiven.

I was ready. I wanted to be saved. Saved from my sin, saved from the emptiness, and saved from the eternal punishment that I deserved. Soon after God blessed me with another new life, I began my new life. I accepted His offer of salvation. Romans 10: 9-10 says, "That if you confess with your mouth, 'Jesus is Lord,' and believe in your heart that God raised him from the dead, you will be saved. For it is with your heart that you believe and are justified, and it is with your mouth that you confess and are saved." (NIV)

I called upon the name of the Lord and asked His forgiveness for my sins. At that very moment, my name was written in the Book of Life and my place in Heaven was assured. I stepped into the waterfall and was completely washed clean by the blood of Jesus Christ, allowing me to come into the presence of God *justified*. It was "just as if I'd never sinned".

Immediately the Holy Spirit came into my life and began to change me from the inside. I had new desires and one of those was the desire to be baptized. I had been baptized as an infant, but it was meaningless. Baptism symbolizes dying to our old self and rising again in Christ. Colossians 2:12 says, "For in baptism you see how your old, evil nature died with him into a new life because you trusted the Word of the mighty God who raised Christ from the dead."

That was what I was professing. I had chosen to give up my old life and live my life for Christ. I had finally made the right choice.

Justin was about five months old when Pastor Curt baptized me. My husband and parents were there to witness my profession of faith. Randal was there also, but simply recalls that the pastor "dunked

Mommy under the water." He didn't understand it yet, but he would because four years later, the same pastor would baptize him.

The battle didn't end when I placed myself in God's hand. Satan didn't like letting go and continued to try to lure me back into his hand. I finally realized that he was the one who wanted me to end my life all of those times when I came close to killing myself. Had he succeeded, he would have had me for eternity. Every time I came close to accepting Christ, he worked extra hard to keep me from making that choice.

I know now that there is a hell and Satan wanted me there—forever. He was the one telling me that I was unworthy of God's love and forgiveness. He was the one reminding me of all of my sins. But the Holy Spirit won out. Once I listened to that still small voice of the Spirit, I knew that God loved me and wanted to forgive me of all of those sins. He wanted me in His hand.

Once I accepted Christ's offer of forgiveness, Satan couldn't take me out of God's hand, but he could still cause me to stumble in my Christian walk. Satan loves to see Christians fall and his lies can be very convincing.

Satan tried to destroy my family by leading me to believe that I should be in control in my marriage and that my children were more important than my husband. But God wanted me to know the truth.

In the young moms' Bible study, we studied a book called *A Woman after God's Own Heart* by Elizabeth George. In that book, George explained that marriage is the foundation of the family and that having a strong marriage results in children who feel safe and secure. Having a solid Christian marriage meant following God's plan. His plan is for the husband to be the leader and for the wife to submit to him.

I struggled with how to submit. For many women, including me, submission has a very negative connotation. But I wanted to try to do it God's way. I knew that His way was best because it had proven to be so in every other area. I fervently read the book and tried to apply what I was reading. I did the best I could to be submissive, allowing Robert to make all of the decisions and deferring to him on everything. Needless to say, he was pleasantly surprised and things seemed to actually improve in our marriage. But he made some decisions that I didn't agree with.

Satan convinced me that my way was better. I gave up on submitting and went back to trying to be in control, even in regards to how many children we would have. Although we had said from the beginning that we would only have two children, I desperately wanted a girl and insisted that we try again. I even got a book called *How to Choose the Sex of Your Baby* and convinced Robert that we should try to have a daughter.

It took longer than with the boys, but we finally got pregnant. I was ecstatic and knew that it would be a girl. I even told the boys that they would be having a sister. (How "in control" did I feel then?) But the excitement didn't last. Blood tests revealed that my hormone levels had dropped. I miscarried. We had to tell the boys that their baby sister was gone.

Randal was very saddened by the news because he really wanted a sister. He asked, "Where is she?"

"She's in Heaven," I responded. It broke my heart when he asked, "Can we go get her?"

When we got pregnant again, we chose not to say anything to anyone until we knew that everything was OK. We were glad we had made that choice, because I miscarried again. I finally realized that I was not in control of this. It was not up to me whether we had another child; it was up to God and it seemed that it was not His will—at least not yet.

We continued to try, but were unable to even achieve a pregnancy for several months. My endometriosis pain had gotten really bad and I was in need of more and more pain medication. My doctor recommended a hysterectomy. I didn't want to give up, but it seemed that I might have to. I was about to consent to the surgery, but then discovered that I was pregnant.

I was elated, but also scared after having two miscarriages in a row. Thankfully all the hormone levels looked great. The lab technician even wondered if I might be having twins. I wasn't, but an ultrasound at twenty weeks revealed that we were having a girl. God chose to bless us with a daughter—in His timing. We named her Sheila.

CHAPTER 9

Led by His hand

God continued to bless us in amazing ways during our time in Grand Island. I had finished my Master's degree in counseling and had begun working as an outpatient mental health therapist. Robert was successful in his job as a high school band director. We had moved into a big house in a nice neighborhood and even had the possibility of paying off our mortgage early. Randal and Justin were in a good school and both were doing well academically. We were happy and comfortable.

But God does not intend for His children to be happy and comfortable in this life. If we are, that means that He's not using us. After a successful seven years in Grand Island, God led both Robert and me to quit our jobs. We obeyed and both of us resigned with no other prospects. We trusted Him to take us where He wanted us to go.

I was offered a job in Omaha where Robert could pursue his Master's degree. Although we had never wanted to live in a big city, we knew that God had led us there. Through my job, I had the opportunity to reach out to many hurting teenagers and to provide some hope to their desperate parents. I took every opportunity to discuss faith and, as a result, I was able to lead a teenage girl to Christ. It was an amazing feeling and I felt honored to be used by God in such a way. I couldn't believe that God would choose to use me after all I had done. But then I realized that God only uses sinners, because we're all sinners.

JULIA KERCHER

Paul is one of my favorite Bible characters. He was as far from Christ as you could imagine. He persecuted and imprisoned Christians and even ordered their execution. His mission was to destroy Christianity. But God reached into his life and changed him. Paul became an extraordinary follower of Christ and led many others to salvation. He wrote many of the books in the New Testament. Through reading about him, I believed that God could use anyone's life, no matter how far they stayed away from Him. He could even use mine.

While in Omaha, our family was given the opportunity to help two sisters who were in need of a home. Their parents' rights had been terminated and they were living in a detention center, partly because of unlawful behaviors, but mostly because they had nowhere else to go. I told Robert about the girls and said that I felt like we were being called to take them into our home. We prayed about it and felt God leading us to become their foster parents. The younger sister was placed with us, but ran away after only three weeks. We didn't know it at the time, but God was preparing us for something He had in store for us in the future.

God also used us to take care of my sister. Janice had been living in Omaha for some time already and was thankful to have us nearby, but she was especially thankful that we were there when her apartment building caught fire. We provided her a place to stay until she could find a new home.

We attended Westside Church where I was able to continue to grow in my new faith. Robert was able to be the primary drummer on their worship team and used his musical talent to worship every week. It was so awesome seeing him play. Watching him reminded me of that Christian band at the youth rally. When you're playing music for God, it's just different.

Of course, the most amazing thing that happened while we were in Omaha was Randal's experience of witnessing to his friend, resulting in Jonah becoming a Christian. Clearly we were meant to be there. But God did not intend for us to stay.

After a year, Robert had earned his Master's degree and was hired by Lincoln Christian School. I was thrilled, especially when I was told that our kids were able to attend for free. I had always wanted them in a Christian school, but we couldn't afford it.

Sadly, however, it was not what we were hoping for. Instead of growing in their faith, both of our sons took huge steps *backward* in their faith while there. We discovered that putting the word "Christian" on a building does not guarantee that everyone in that building is a Christian. Being immersed in God's Word does not ensure that the Message will sink in and the ability to recite Bible verses does not mean that the students are learning to live by those words. Just as I had experienced at the Baptist church I attended as a teenager, our sons found themselves surrounded by hypocrisy.

Randal was no longer witnessing to kids. In fact, he was interacting with them as little as possible. Many of the kids at the Christian school had allowed themselves to be tainted by the world. Instead of appreciating the safety of being in a Christian environment, they took every opportunity possible to experience the sinful pleasures of this world. They listened to secular music, played violent video games, and told crude jokes. They were allowing themselves to be influenced by the very things that their parents were trying to shelter them from. I wondered how it could be that people who claim to be Christians could behave in such non-Christian ways.

Please don't get me wrong here. There were some great Christian kids in that school and our boys were grateful for every one of them. But there were some who could certainly be described as hypocrites. I share this experience not to bash the school, but to urge Christians *everywhere* to act like Christians. Our boys survived and eventually their faith grew again, but I have to wonder how many others ended up leaving the faith due to similar experiences. It's our responsibility as Christians not only to lead people to Christ, but also to demonstrate Christ to them in our ongoing interactions.

I've since learned that surveys indicate a primary reason many people reject Christianity is because of people who call themselves Christians. Instead of pouring out the sweet taste of the Holy Spirit, too many Christians are pouring out something else and, instead of leaving you hungry for more, it just leaves a bad taste in your mouth. Another children's message I gave at church, after my Coke can demonstration, illustrated the "taste" of hypocrisy.

I held up a bottle of Aquafina and explained that it is clean and pure like the Holy Spirit. It is refreshing to drink and quenches the thirst. Then, I added a little vinegar to the water and said, "This is what happens when we let sin come in. It permeates the water and makes it bitter. It's no longer pure. It's tainted and not pleasant to drink. It leaves a bad taste in your mouth."

The school left a bad taste in our mouths. Home schooling seemed like a better option. But I was working full-time and didn't have the time or the energy to home-school. We asked Randal to stick it out, hoping that things would get better.

Unfortunately the rest of the year didn't go any better for him—or for me. Although I had been doing better after Sheila's birth, my endometriosis pain returned and again became unbearable. I planned to have a total hysterectomy as soon as I could save up enough sick time. But God had other plans. Before I could get the surgery scheduled, I discovered that I was pregnant.

We hadn't been trying for a fourth child, but I was thrilled by this unexpected gift. I really wanted two boys and two girls—and that was exactly what I got. After spending a few weeks on bed rest, I gave birth to our second daughter, Kiriana, whom we call "Kiri". The sick time I was saving up for a hysterectomy was used for maternity leave.

When I returned to work, my mother came to take care of Kiri so she wouldn't have to go to daycare. Although it was hard leaving my baby at home, God was able to use me in my job. He gave me the opportunity to reach out to some really lost and hurting kids. I was able to share my faith with many of them and more than one came to a saving faith in Christ. I knew that He was the only One who could heal their pain and transform their lives. It was heartbreaking when others chose to continue to go their own way because I knew where that path would take them. I'd been there. I continued to pray for them that they would make the right choice like Randal and Justin had.

Justin accepted Jesus as his Savior at a young age and did his best to be obedient in his walk with Christ, but he had hesitated to be baptized. The summer after Kiri's birth, there was an announcement in the church bulletin that they would be baptizing people at the local water park. Justin was then ready to profess his faith.

The pastor gave Justin the option to be baptized by anyone he wanted. He chose his father and me. It was an incredible honor. I was so glad to know that both of my son's had made the right choice. They were both in God's hand and I prayed that, unlike me, they would choose to stay there.

The following school year, Randal was also doing better. He even began to like school somewhat. Justin had made one genuine friend and things looked like they were going along nicely for a change. We were getting "comfortable." But remember, if we're comfortable, that means that God isn't using us. God planned to use us.

The school administration made some budget cuts that included reducing the band director position to half time. We considered options to be able to stay, but God soon made it clear that it was time to go. We had no idea what the future would be for us, but we could be at peace knowing that God knew. We could rest in the safety of His hand until he revealed His plan. After a few months of uncertainty, He did.

I saw a news article on the front page of the newspaper. The new band director just hired at Falls City, Nebraska had suddenly died. I knew that it would be difficult for them to find a replacement at such a late date. Robert was in western Nebraska on his two-week annual training with the National Guard. When I told him about what I had read, he asked me to write his cover letter and update his resume. I did so and sent them off that very day.

The next evening I prayed, "God, I don't care where we go. Just tell us where You want us to be." I then walked by the computer and felt compelled to check my e-mail. There it was, an e-mail from the principal at Falls City High School. He wanted to schedule an interview with Robert. I knew right then that we would be moving to Falls City.

My parents were visiting at the time and I went upstairs and told my mother, "God just sent me an e-mail." She had been worrying that Robert would not find a job. I showed her the message and told her that God was taking care of us.

Robert drove across the state a few days later for the interview. Wearing his Army uniform, he was immediately the talk of the town. Needless to say, he was offered the position. I knew that this was where God wanted us to be.

After his Guard training, Robert and the older kids were committed to helping his parents put a new roof on their cabin in Colorado. We needed to find a house, so my dad took care of young Kiri while Mom and I made the one hundred mile journey to Falls City to look for a home.

We had been at it for the better part of the day and still had nothing that would work for us. But Mom is stubborn and insisted that we stop at another realtor's office before heading back. They were able to get us into one last house that the other realtor couldn't. It was a four-bedroom, two-story house for only $50,000. It was really dirty and smelled bad, but for only $50, 000, I knew that I could clean it up. I said, "We'll take it." With my parents' help, we bought it with cash. No mortgage payments meant that I would be able to stay home with Kiri.

We placed our other house on the market as soon as we knew we were moving, but it had not sold yet. We couldn't afford to keep making the payments, so we put it up for rent. Once again, God took care of us. The parents of one of Robert's students had just been told that they needed to move out of their rental house. They wanted to be close to the school, which our house was. They moved in as we moved out.

Our new renters just happened to be friends with our former small group leaders from the E-Free church in Grand Island. They told us that Chuck and Julie had moved to Falls City four years ago. We planned to look them up after we moved. But we wouldn't have to wait.

CHAPTER 10

"You want us to do *what*?"

When we pulled into the driveway of our new house, Chuck and Julie were waiting to help us unload the U-Haul along with several other people that we didn't even know. We were amazed and thankful for the friendliness of the small town.

We were also excited to reconnect with Chuck and Julie. Since they had the same beliefs that we did, we knew that wherever they were going to church would be the right church for us. We were shocked when they told us that in the four years that they had been in Falls City, they had not found a church home. We were on our own again to find a body of believers.

We began searching for a church that offered sound Biblical teaching and a modern worship style. Although we were hesitant to try it, we went to the Pentecostal church and found that we liked it a lot. In looking over the church's doctrine, we found that we agreed with everything except their practice of speaking in tongues. We asked the pastor if we could still worship there if we did not believe in this practice and he assured us that we could.

We prayed about it for some time and felt like Good News was where we were supposed to be. Chuck and Julie then started attending there too. Robert became the drummer on the worship team and I taught a parenting class during the Sunday School hour. It felt good to be so involved because we had not done that at previous churches we attended. We wanted to do more for the church—and for the community.

I had taught parenting classes in the past and wanted to do so again when we moved to Falls City. I contacted the director of the community mental health center to inquire about offering a class. That phone call led to me not only teaching a parenting class, but also working for them as a part-time therapist one day a week.

I was able to share my faith often and utilized Christian counseling with anyone who was open to it. I finally began to recognize God's awesome power and opened myself to be His vessel. Through me, God was able to heal a broken marriage and reach out to a lost teenager. I was amazed at the power that was available to me when I chose to plug in to it. On my own, I was a mediocre therapist. With God leading me, so much more healing took place.

Not only was God leading me, He was leading Robert also. Shortly before Christmas, Robert suggested that we have our nieces and nephew come for a visit. I was quite surprised at the suggestion since we rarely spent time with my sister and brother-in-law and their three children.

Jill's husband, Tim, was also visually impaired due to a congenital disorder. They had three children, but were unable to properly care for them. The kids had been removed and placed in foster care more than once due to unsanitary living conditions. I was really shocked when Robert said that maybe we could be their foster parents if they needed to be removed again. I knew that it must be God leading him to say these things, so I said, "OK, I'll give them a call."

Tim and Jill agreed to let the kids come and we arranged a three-day visit during Christmas break. I drove to Nebraska City to pick them up on New Year's Day.

When I entered the home to get the children, I was completely aghast by what I saw. It was the worst I had ever seen it. I can't even describe how bad it was. All I wanted to do was grab the kids and get them out of there. Tim and Jill seemed completely unaware of the problem.

As we walked out to the van, Tim mentioned that the family was being investigated by Child Protective Services due to a report that their oldest son, Levi, was malnourished. I knew that if CPS saw the condition of the home as it was, the children would most certainly be removed. I encouraged Tim and Jill to clean it up while the kids were with us. I also told them that if the kids did need to be placed out of their home, Robert and I would take them. They were grateful for the offer.

As I drove to Falls City with the children, I wondered if I would be taking them back. Three days later, I had my answer. A caseworker from CPS called to inform us that the home was deemed to be unfit for the children to return. We were asked to keep them. Of course, we agreed to do so and then knew why God had given us that experience as foster parents in Omaha. He was preparing us for this. That previous experience, however, did not prepare us for taking in three special needs kids in addition to four of our own. But God provided for us through it all.

We received no foster care payment for several weeks and didn't know how we would afford to feed everyone. While I was in the kitchen one evening preparing supper, a woman from my Bible study group and her husband came to the door carrying boxes of groceries. I broke down and cried in thankfulness for their generosity and in shame for doubting. God placed those children in our home and He would provide for them through His people. Our church and Bible study families provided us with more groceries, furniture, clothing, and pretty much everything we needed. We were overwhelmed with gratitude and never felt alone even for a moment.

Although we could feed and clothe everyone, after about a month, it was apparent that we could not care for Angel any longer. She was six years old at the time, but she was functioning more on the level of a two-year-old. We didn't know how to help her and her behaviors were causing then two-year-old Kiri to regress. It was a hard decision, but we knew that we had to do what was best for her and us. We had to ask to have Angel placed with another family.

God's hand went before us again and a family from our church agreed to take her in. They immediately loved her. She bonded to them and flourished. We were able to still see her every week at church and were truly amazed at how happy she was and how quickly she progressed.

We were still overwhelmed with six children, but committed to care for Levi and Kayelee at least until the end of the school year. We believed that God would provide other homes for them also. So we waited until he revealed those families.

Kayelee's special education teacher began taking her out to their farm after school. Soon after that, she said that she and her husband were interested in becoming Kayelee's foster parents. They began the process of becoming approved for foster care and Kayelee began spending a lot more time with them in preparation to move in after the end of the school year.

But Levi didn't have another placement yet. I knew he would be difficult to place because he had a lot of issues, including an eating disorder that made every mealtime a battle. I began to worry, but then I got a call from our pastor's wife. They had been praying about it and felt God leading them to take Levi into their family.

We were amazed and knew that God was taking care of these children. All of them would be in good, loving homes in the same community. They would be able to see one another, but also get the extra attention that they each needed. When the school year ended, Levi and Kayelee moved into their new homes and we were back to four.

I continued to work one day a week, although I had cut back on my hours because of the demands of the foster children, but I began feeling God telling me that I needed to quit. I would feel anxiety every morning when I had to go to work and for most of the time while I was there. I really wanted to quit, but I felt pressure to stay to get that extra paycheck. God then made the choice clear.

Robert was preparing to leave for his two-week annual training with the National Guard and he needed to wash his uniforms. Before I left for work that morning, he had asked me if I needed anything laundered. I asked him to wash our new set of sheets. A few hours later, he called me at work and asked, "Hey, uh how do I get red dye out of my uniforms?"

Our new sheets were burgundy and not colorfast. He had thrown them in with his uniforms. That clinched it. I knew that I should have been the one doing the laundry. I left early that day and figured out how to save the uniforms, and therefore a few hundred dollars. I quit the following week and returned to being a full-time wife and mother.

After our nieces and nephew left our home, we continued attending the Pentecostal church, but the tongues speaking became an issue. We couldn't invite anyone to church for fear that someone would start speaking in tongues and we would have to try to explain something that we didn't even believe in.

One Sunday, a visiting pastor came and gave the sermon. He talked about tongues and at the end of his message, he made an alter call for anyone in the congregation who had not been "filled with the Holy Spirit" to come up front. Sheila, who was six at the time and had taken Christ as her Savior, whispered to me, "Mama, have I been filled?" I assured her that she had and we left the church, never to return.

Please understand. I am not saying by any means that Pentecostals are not Christian. They simply have a certain practice that makes many people uncomfortable. It made us uncomfortable enough that we could no longer worship there.

Chuck and Julie left the church at the same time and the following week we drove to Sabetha, Kansas to attend a non-denominational church called "NorthRidge." It was a 25-minute drive each way, but it was worth it. The church reminded us all of the E-Free Church we had attended in Grand Island. They had contemporary music and were completely Bible-based with no uncomfortable practices. We knew this was the right place for us.

Yet it was hard for us to leave Good News because we loved the people there. We found a way to maintain contact through a small group with the pastor and several members of the church. Together we studied *Experiencing God* by Henry and Richard Blackaby and Claude King. In a section titled, "Knowing Where God Is at Work" we were asked to write in the margin ideas about how we could begin to watch for God's activity around us and join Him. We wrote:

Evangelical Church in Falls City
Minister to Kayelee

Chuck and Julie had been talking to the pastor at NorthRidge about having a satellite church in Falls City. Pastor Charlie was open to the idea and we joined them in discussing possibilities to make it happen. Several families in Falls City were driving to Sabetha every week to go to church. We knew that there were many more families in Falls City that didn't go to church at all. We really wanted to reach them.

In addition to reaching the un-churched, we also wanted to ensure that Kayelee had a sound spiritual upbringing. Her foster parents were Catholic and she was becoming confused. She had been raised Baptist. Tim and Jill had indicated that, if they were not able to have the kids back, they wanted them in a Protestant Christian home. We started having Kayelee stay with us on Saturday nights and go to church with us at NorthRidge on Sundays. Before long, it was apparent that God wanted us to do more than just provide a spiritual upbringing for Kayelee.

CHAPTER 11

Pray Until Something Happens

As time went on, it looked more and more like Tim and Jill's parental rights would be terminated. Kayelee's foster parents decided that they could not keep her long-term and they were not interested in adopting her. We knew we couldn't let her go to strangers, so she began spending entire weekends with us while we determined whether we should take her back in.

Our girls looked forward to Kayelee's visits and Robert was open to the idea of taking her back, but I was hesitant. Satan had not given up on trying to destroy our marriage. Robert and I had not been getting along well. We argued—a lot. There were times when I wasn't even sure that our marriage would last. We were struggling with parenting our own four children and adding a fifth didn't seem to make much sense. I hadn't yet accepted that what God asks us to do rarely makes any sense to us. That's how we know it's from Him. Instead I found myself questioning God. And as I had learned in the *Experiencing God* study, when we question God, He answers.

One night after Robert and I had been arguing, I went to bed alone. I cried out to God, "Why did You even put us together? We have absolutely nothing in common. All we do is argue. How can we take Kayelee in when we can't even agree on how to raise our own kids?"

I also asked God, "Why did You tell me to quit my job? I'm going crazy being home with Kiri all day every day."

I laid alone in the dark for several minutes, crying out to God in my mind. I knew that God always answers prayer, so I prayed as fervently as I had ever prayed. Some time before that, I had heard of the acronym, "PUSH". It stands for "Pray Until Something Happens". That was what I did. I prayed until something happened—God answered me!

I had never had the ability to close my eyes and truly picture anything. Never before could I think of something and see an image of it in my mind. I had certainly never seen an image of something I wasn't even thinking about. But while lying there with my eyes closed, I saw the clear image of a tiger. I then saw a marching band and, next, a football team. It all seemed very strange to me and I quickly dismissed it, until Robert came into the room and spoke.

He said, "I know you're upset, but can I talk to you about something?" He shared with me that he had been struggling with how to talk to the football coaches about scheduling football practices and events at the same time as band practice. The Falls City school mascot is the tiger.

What I had just seen suddenly made perfect sense. I believed that God had allowed me to see what my husband was thinking in order to show me that He put me with this man for a purpose—to be *his* helper. I was able to assist Robert in coming up with a way to talk to the coaches.

After that, I felt better about our relationship. I was ready to obey God and have Kayelee move in with us. I was more relaxed and closed my eyes to go to sleep. But before sleep came, I saw another vision. Again I saw images in my mind, but these were not as clear as before.

I saw what looked like a silver colored vehicle going down a highway and slamming into something. It was so real that I could sense the impact. I then saw an empty grey seat covered with dust or some other kind of debris. Next, I saw a hospital bed. I could only see the foot of the bed, so I couldn't tell who was in it. The last image really shook me. It was the image of a casket.

My entire body became tense and I felt myself screaming inside. All I wanted to do was to wake up from this horrible nightmare. But there was no waking up. I wasn't sleeping. I was wide awake and clearly seeing a vision from God.

I believed that through that vision, God was answering my second question. He was allowing me to experience what I would feel if I lost Kiri, or any of my children. I immediately got out of bed and went to the girls' room. I sat next to Kiri's bed and caressed her as she slept. I vowed to try to be a better mother to her and to her siblings.

After what I had just experienced, I wasn't ready to go to sleep right away, so I went downstairs and checked my e-mail. We had gone to our former church in Lincoln the prior weekend and I had written a prayer request on a communication card. I wrote that I was struggling with my faith, my marriage, and my kids. I received this e-mail response from the pastor:

> Julia,
>
> I prayed for you tonight and will continue to do so. I'm so sorry that you have been struggling with your faith, marriage and your kids. Please know of my prayers and support. If I may be of any help, please let me know. I would be honored to be of support. Regardless, I will commit to pray for you and your family.
>
> Tim

I looked at the time he had sent the e-mail. He was praying for me exactly at the time I was experiencing the visions!

The next day, I tried to show Kiri how much I appreciated her and spent more time with her. A few days later, I told Robert and the other children about the vision. I even shared it with our small group. It was certainly an example of "experiencing God". The vision had such an impact on me that I wanted to let others know about it.

A few days later, I had another strange experience. I was again feeling trapped in my marriage and wanted out. I was lying awake in bed, wishing I had never married the man lying next to me. I eventually drifted off to sleep only to be awakened soon after by the need to go to the bathroom.

I quietly slipped out of bed and tried to make my way to the door. The room seemed unusually dark. There was no light coming in from the windows and the only thing I could see was the digital clock over the bed. I walked to the door, as I had done countless times before, and reached for the doorknob. But I couldn't find it. I slid my hand up and down the door, but there was no knob.

I looked back at the clock above the bed to orient me and know if I was at the right door since we had two leading out of our bedroom. I determined that I was at the correct door and I knew that the knob should be right where my hand was, but it wasn't. I reached out my left hand and felt the wall just as I expected. I knew that the doorknob was on the right side of the door furthest from the wall. I felt my way back across the door and reached the doorframe. Again I slid my hand up and down, feeling for the knob. But the door was completely smooth. It was as though the knob had disappeared.

I was pretty freaked out and decided that I didn't need to use the bathroom that badly after all. I got back in bed and tried to sleep, hoping that the knob would return by morning.

The next day, there was light coming in from the windows and the doorknob that was not there the night before was once again visible. I told my family about the experience and they all thought I was crazy. They teased me for some time about the "disappearing doorknob", so I didn't share the experience with anyone else. I did, however, tell my mother about the vision.

I had been feeling God leading me to witness to my mother for some time. She and Dad were still attending the Lutheran church where they didn't talk much about the Bible and not at all about salvation. I knew she was as lost and confused as I was a few years earlier. She had come to Julie's Bible study with me a few times when she and Dad visited and she was starting to understand more.

It was during that Bible study a few weeks later that the experience with the missing doorknob finally made sense. We listened to a CD that evening from a series called, "House or Home". Chip Ingram spoke on "Marriage—A Holy Covenant". He said that when we get married, we should picture it like entering a small brick room with no backdoor. Once you and your spouse are in, the door behind you is bricked over. There is no way out, so you have to find a way to work things out.

I knew then that God had made that doorknob disappear. I figured that if He could create an entire universe out of nothing, He could surely make a doorknob disappear for a few minutes if He wants to. He was telling me something through that experience. He was telling me that I needed to stop looking for a way out of my marriage. I needed to accept that, even though I was not in God's hand when we met, Robert was. He led Robert to me. He brought us together and He wanted us to stay together. No, Robert is not perfect, but neither am I. If God can forgive me for my mistakes and continue to love and accept me in spite of them, surely I can do the same for Robert. That was what God was calling me to do. He knew that our marriage needed to be strong because we were in store for a tremendous storm that would either strengthen us or tear us apart.

CHAPTER 12

The vision revealed

A few months before having the visions, I felt God leading me to write a book. I hadn't started because I didn't know what He wanted me to write about. I decided that the visions would be a good starting place, so on November 10, 2009 I began writing. On that day I wrote:

I don't know if this was a vision of the future or simply a way to show me something.

Just over a month later, it all became clear. God had shown me the immediate future when He showed me what Robert was about to tell me. He wanted to let me know that what I was about to see next was also from Him and it was also a glimpse into the future.

I was awakened on December 14, 2009, to the sound of the phone ringing. The school's automated calling system informed me that school had been postponed until 10:00 AM due to icy road conditions. I was relieved because it was my first day as a substitute teacher. I had another couple of hours to prepare. Part of me wished that they would cancel school for the entire day, but I knew that if they did, they would also have to postpone the Middle School concert that was scheduled for that evening. My parents were coming to Falls City for the concert. They were also going to stay with Kiri that afternoon.

Moments later, Mom called from Lincoln and said, "We're thinking of just heading west."

Mom never liked to drive in bad weather. They were considering going back home to Holdrege since the roads were better that way, but I hated for them to miss the concert. I suggested that they give it some time and see if the roads got better. At 9:00, she called again and said that they were on their way. They would stop in Nebraska City to see Jill and Tim and then meet us for lunch at Subway at 12:20.

At about 9:30, I loaded the kids into the van to get them all to their respective schools. First we would drop Kiri of at her new sitter's home.

We knew Pat from when we had attended Good News. She was a sweet older woman who adored kids. We knew that we would really miss seeing her when we quit attending the church. But Pat hosted the *Experiencing God* study in her home, so we got to see her for a few more weeks.

One evening, I mentioned to Pat that I was thinking of being a substitute teacher, but I didn't have anyone to watch Kiri. She said that she would be thrilled to take care of her. I knew that God was providing for my need so I graciously accepted her offer. This would be the first day that Pat would watch Kiri, which was why my parents were going to keep her for the afternoon. I knew that she would not nap well in a strange place. Since school was postponed, she would only be at Pat's for a few hours.

Pat's driveway had a steep slope and, because it was still icy, I wasn't able to make it to the top. I gave up and stopped the van midway up. It felt stable, so I placed it in park and got out. But as I prepared to open Kiri's door, the van started to slide down the driveway. I felt completely helpless as I saw the girls inside screaming and panicking. I didn't know what to do other than to grab the door handle and stay with it.

Fourteen-year-old Randal was sitting in the front seat and knew which one was the brake pedal. He leaned over and pushed the pedal, amazingly bringing the van to a stop. I thanked God for Randal's quick reflexes as I carefully climbed in and backed the van to the street. I decided it would be best to walk Kiri to the house on the grass.

After that excitement, I felt even less prepared for my first day as a substitute teacher at the high school. Although the first class went reasonably well, the second one was the longest fifty minutes of my life. One student was particularly challenging and I finally said to him, "Look, this is my first day subbing and I really don't want to have to send anyone to the office. Do you think we could just make it through the next twenty minutes?" He didn't cause any further problems. I wish I could say the same for the rest of the class. Let's just say I was glad when it was over. And since it had been a late start, it was already time for lunch.

Kiri and I arrived at Subway at 12:15. I ordered a pizza for her, but decided I would wait to get my own lunch until Mom and Dad got there. Robert arrived just after 12:20. My parents weren't there yet and I was getting a little concerned. When it got to be 12:30 and they were still not there, I was really worried. My parents were rarely ever late and, if they were going to be, they always called. I just knew something was wrong.

I called Mom's cell phone. It rang several times, but there was no answer. I figured that maybe they were in an area with no service. There were a lot of those areas between Nebraska City and Falls City. So I gave it a few minutes and tried again. Still no answer. This time I left a message.

"Hey, we're at Subway. You're not here and I am getting really worried. Please call me as soon as you get this message." As I closed my phone, I prayed. *Please, God, please let them be OK.*

Kiri wasn't going to be able to eat all of her pizza, so I took a piece and tried to eat. I kept looking out the window, hoping to see my parents' car pull into the parking lot. Then my phone rang. I was so relieved and looked at the display, expecting to see Mom's number on the screen. Instead it was Tim. I figured that maybe he was calling to tell me that Mom and Dad had gotten a late start or perhaps that they had forgotten something. Instead he asked, "Has the sheriff contacted you yet?"

My heart sank and I knew that something really bad had happened. I said, "No, why?" not really wanting to hear the answer.

He said, "Your parents were in a car accident."

My fears had been confirmed. But nothing could have prepared me for what Tim said next.

"Your dad died."

"What?!" I felt as though my heart had just been ripped out of my chest. "No! NO, that can't be!"

I didn't want to believe it. There had to be some mistake. Dad couldn't possibly be dead. They must have the wrong car or the wrong person. Maybe they just thought he was dead, but he could still be revived. Maybe he's just in a coma, or I don't know what. I just knew that he couldn't possibly be gone. I refused to let him go. *Not Daddy, oh God, please, not him!*

Tim went on to say, "Your mom is in serious condition. They're transporting her by ambulance . . ." My head was spinning and I couldn't listen to him. All I could do was shake my head and cry, "No, no, no, no-o-o-o!"

I was in absolute agony. I can't even describe the intense emotion that I felt at that moment. I felt all of the same pain and anguish that I felt when I had seen the vision. The tightness in my stomach, the tension in my entire body, but it was ten times worse.

All of those old feelings that I had before becoming a Christian came rushing back. The feeling that God is punishing and that He doesn't really care about us. After all that had happened in the past few years, how much I had grown in my faith, how we had trusted God in everything, I could not understand why God would do this to me. I could not understand why He would take Dad. It made no sense to me.

Then I was hit with the feeling that I was responsible. I believed that the accident was all my fault, that I actually had some control over things and that my actions, or inactions, had led to the crash.

If only I had let them go back home like Mom wanted. If only I hadn't agreed to sub today, they wouldn't have been in such a hurry to get here. If only I had called Mom when I knew how icy it still was. If only . . .

Then I went into the questioning. *Why, God, why? Why would you take him?*

Did I actually think that my decision to become a Christian somehow made me immune to pain and suffering? Of course not. My life had not gotten easier since becoming a Christian. In fact in many ways, it had gotten harder. I had to give up my desire to be in control and trust in Someone else. Psalms 23:4 says, "Even when walking through the dark valley of death I will not be afraid, for You are close beside me, guarding, guiding me all the way." I knew that God was with me at all times and that He could guide me because He knew what was going to happen.

It was then that I recalled the vision and it was suddenly very clear. I had assumed that the silver vehicle was our van. But my parents' car was also silver. It was their car that I had seen. It was Mom in the hospital bed and it was Dad in the casket. God had shown me the future in that vision, but only an unclear glimpse. Had it been clear, I would have tried to do something to change it. But there was nothing I could have done. God had already planned it. Although I didn't understand it, I had to trust in Him that there was a reason. But at that moment, that was really hard to do.

Robert took the phone and wrote down all of the information. I slumped down in the seat, bawling and crying out to God. When we arrived home, he called the hospital and confirmed that Dad had indeed died in the accident. When I heard that Daddy was really gone, the anguish intensified. Not only did I still blame myself for the accident, but I also believed that I might never see my father again.

CHAPTER 13

"Was he saved?"

Although Dad had become very involved in the church after I moved away from home, I was uncertain of his salvation. I knew that there were plenty of people who attended church "religiously", but were not saved. I was one of them for a long time. I had tried many times to talk to Dad about salvation, but he just never wanted to discuss it. He didn't even want to be around when I would talk to Mom about faith.

I recalled one occasion when Mom and I were having a deep discussion about salvation. Dad left the room as usual. I confronted him later and asked, "Where are you at with this?"

He answered, "I don't know," and walked away.

That event came to the forefront of my memory. I became so angry with myself for letting him go. *I should have pushed him further.* I just figured that we would talk about it another time. But that other time never came. Now he was gone and it was too late. The regret that I felt was incredible.

Mom had come to some understanding of salvation through Bible studies and my witnessing to her. However she never felt like she could share her newfound knowledge with Dad. They were still going to church together and had even started attending an adult Sunday School class, but they never talked about faith issues together. I knew that she would feel the same regret that I was feeling. But we wouldn't be able to talk about it anytime soon.

Mom had suffered significant facial injuries in the accident. She also had a collapsed lung and had to be intubated. They were transporting her by ambulance to a trauma center in Lincoln.

When I called the hospital to see if Mom had arrived, I was told that she had not. I got that sinking feeling again. I knew that some of the roads were still icy and I feared the worst. I sat and prayed. *Please, God, please don't take her, too. I cannot handle losing them both.*

God answered that prayer. When I called the hospital again, I was told that Mom had arrived. They were admitting her to the intensive care unit where she would remain sedated for at least a day or two. I told the nurse that we probably would not come until the next day because of the road conditions. She understood and said that I could call as often as I wanted to check on her.

After I hung up the phone, I stood in the kitchen, still trying to make sense of it all. Robert came in, wrapped his arms around me, and asked, "What can I do for you?"

I shook my head and said, "Wake me up. Just wake me up and tell me this is all just a bad dream." I buried my head in his chest and began to cry. Robert wrapped his arms around me and held me tight. I wanted to stay there safe in his arms and just bawl, but then the phone rang. I had to break free to answer it.

It was the hospital chaplain. She filled me in a little more on Mom's condition and asked when we were coming. I said, "We're waiting until tomorrow when the roads are better."

She said, "We usually ask family to come right away in these instances."

Her words frightened me. I began to think that I might lose Mom too. I couldn't bear to have that happen, but if it was going to, I needed to see her first. Four years earlier, my grandmother died. We got the first flight we could when we knew that she didn't have much time left. I prayed the whole way there that she would hang on until we arrived. But we were too late. Aunt Kathy met us at the baggage claim with tears in her eyes and said, "She's gone." Grandma had died minutes before we arrived.

Grandma had also never wanted to talk about faith. I had tried many times, but she would get angry. I didn't get the chance to talk to her before her death to be absolutely assured of her salvation. I've regretted that ever since. Although Mom had indicated an understanding of salvation, I was uncertain of whether or not she had taken that step. I decided that I needed to go.

Robert agreed and went to pick up the kids from their schools. But right after he left, Tim called and told me that the roads were still bad. I knew that it didn't make sense to risk my life to go. I had to trust God to take care of her until I could get there tomorrow. I called Robert and told him that I was not going to go. He said that he would go ahead and get the kids out early anyway since he was already there.

While I was waiting for them to get home, I thought of Pastor Tim in Lincoln. I called and told him about the accident. I asked him to go to the hospital and pray over Mom. Prayer was the only power I had then. I prayed that Mom would be OK and I began praying for Dad, begging God to tell me where he was.

When the kids arrived, they had no idea what was going on. Justin saw my red and swollen face and asked, "Is it something bad?"

I nodded. It took me a moment to get the words out and I didn't know how to say it. I took a deep breath and said, "Grandma and Grandpa were in an accident."

Sheila was sitting next to me and asked, "Are they dead?"

I closed my eyes and tried to hold back the tears. It was so hard to speak the words because it made it that much more real. I finally said, "Grandpa is . . .and Grandma is in the hospital."

Sheila immediately broke down and started crying. I held her and tried to comfort her, but all I could do was cry right along with her. Justin also began to cry, but through the tears he said something I will never forget, something amazingly profound for an 11-year-old. He said, "God gives and God takes away." He recalled one of our family's favorite songs, "Blessed Be Your Name," by Tree 63.

He gives and takes away, He gives and takes away.
My heart will choose to say, Lord blessed be Your name.

Already at his young age, Justin understood that everything and everyone we have in our lives here on earth is temporary. He also understood that God is in control and we are to trust in Him in both the good times and the bad.

Then Justin asked a question that I did not want to answer. "Was he saved?"

I so wanted to reassure him and spare him the anguish that I was feeling. But he knew as well as I did that Grandpa didn't talk about faith. I've never liked lying to my kids, so I answered, "I don't know for sure."

More tears fell and soon all three of us were sobbing. But Randal just sat in silence, looking at the floor. Robert then spoke up and said, "I want both of you boys to know that it's OK to cry. Your grandfather was a good man and I'm going to miss him dearly."

Robert sat down and began to cry. Then Randal finally let the tears fall.

The rest of the afternoon was a blur. There were so many phone calls that I did not want to make, so many family members I had to tell. It didn't get any easier with each one.

I also received a lot of calls that I was not prepared to handle. The funeral home director wanted to know what to do with Dad's body. I didn't know. Then I remembered that Mom had given me paperwork outlining her and Dad's final wishes years before. I hadn't looked at it at the time because I didn't want to think about them dying. Now I was glad to have it.

I retrieved the envelope from the file drawer and looked for Dad's papers. I saw that he wanted to donate his body to the State Anatomical Board. I made several phone calls to try to carry out his final wishes, but was informed that they would not be able take his body because of the severity of his injuries. I asked the funeral home to hold onto his body until I could talk to Mom. They said they could keep it for up to three days.

After the numerous phone calls, I arrived late for the concert and had to park a block away. By the time I got there, the sixth grade band had already performed. I had missed seeing Justin play his saxophone. The junior high band was next, so at least I would get to see Randal playing the drums. But it was really hard to focus on the music. My mind wasn't there and I don't even remember the first two songs. But then came the third.

Robert announced, "This song has special meaning for me tonight. My father-in-law died in a car accident this morning." The song was titled "Dona Nobis Pacem", meaning "Grant Us Peace". Tears streamed down my face as the band played like I had never heard them play before. Later Robert told me that he didn't know why he had chosen that song for the concert. It was certainly not a Christmas song. Everything that didn't make sense at the time was all becoming clear.

As I left the school, I had to walk that block back to my van. Dad always loved to walk and I thought of him as I made my way down the street. Suddenly I felt his presence. It felt as though he was walking right beside me. Then I felt his arms around me, holding me and comforting me like he used to do. Again the tears flowed. I began to believe that maybe Dad really was in Heaven and he was trying to assure me of this. I wanted so badly to believe that. I needed to believe that. But I still wasn't absolutely certain. I continued to pray.

CHAPTER 14

The godly shall rest in peace

Sleep did not come easy that night. I stayed awake for hours praying. I continued to beg God to let me know where my father was. *Please, God, please let me know. I need to know for sure if I will see him again. Please tell me.*

Finally, at around 2 AM, I got out of bed and went downstairs. I was drawn to the only thing that had ever consistently given me answers. I picked up my Bible.

Most of the time I read my Bible by simply opening it to wherever God leads me. It had worked for me many other times when I needed His guidance. Before opening it, I prayed, *Please, God, please tell me what I need to know.* I then opened the Bible to the book of Isaiah. Right at the top of the page I read this heading:

The godly shall rest in peace

Tears immediately filled my eyes and I knew that God had answered my question. Through the tears, I read the first two verses of Isaiah 57.

The good men perish; the godly die before their time and no one seems to care or wonder why. No one seems to realize that God is taking them away from evil days ahead. For the godly who die shall rest in peace.

I whispered, "Thank You, thank You, God, thank You." I broke down and wept, tears falling on the pages of my Bible. But these were no longer tears of pain or anguish. These were tears of joy and gratitude. The joy of knowing for absolute certain that my father is in Heaven and that I will one day see him again and gratitude toward God for answering my prayers and providing me with that assurance.

I know that many people believe that the Bible was written thousands of years ago and therefore has no relevance to us today. That is simply not true. God uses His Word to speak to us today. It was no coincidence that I turned to that page. God was speaking to me to answer my question. He was telling me that the accident wasn't a punishment and it wasn't my fault. It was His plan. He planned long ago to take Dad home in that way at that time to spare him from the evil days to come.

I went back upstairs and woke Sheila to have her use the bathroom. I shared with her what God had just told me. She was thrilled. Kiri woke up when we came back into the room and she asked me to come and sit with her for a while. I was happy to do so. I sat on the floor next to Kiri's bed and caressed her hair. Instantly I recalled being in that exact position after seeing my vision. I realized then that God wasn't warning me that I might lose Kiri. He was showing me that we would be comforting one another at this time.

Kiri asked me to turn on the CD player. Just a few nights before, we had changed the CD from kids' songs to Christian worship songs and I was so grateful. Every song on that CD spoke to me and provided me with amazing comfort and encouragement. It was just one more way that God had prepared things ahead of time.

One of the things that was most difficult for us about moving to Falls City was the lack of Christian radio. When Randal was about two or three years old, we switched away from secular radio because we didn't want him repeating the lyrics of some of the songs he was hearing. Since then, we have come to love and appreciate Christian music. Listening to lyrics that are uplifting and encouraging has such a profound impact on our mood and demeanor. As I stated earlier, what you put into your mind really affects you.

The next morning, I was able to assure Justin without a doubt that Grandpa was saved and is now in Heaven. He was so grateful and his mood changed immediately. He now knew that Grandpa was not gone; he just wouldn't be able to see him for a while. But one day he would again and that was all he needed.

I began to look back on Dad's life and wondered when he was saved. For as long as I could remember, Dad was incredibly kind, loving, loyal, and generous. Yet I knew that none of those qualities could result in salvation and that even kind and generous people can be lost and separated from God. Nothing he could do could earn him salvation. Ephesians 2:8-9 says, "For it is by grace you have been saved, through faith—and this not from yourselves, it is the gift of God—not by works, so that no one can boast." (NIV) Dad had to choose to accept salvation. He could not earn it. Good works don't grant us a place in Heaven. My father could only be saved by trusting Jesus and placing his life in God's hand.

Then I recalled that last summer he and Mom went to Maine for Dad's class reunion and a visit with Kathy. They had lunch with his cousin, Barbara, whom many family members described as a "born again Christian". I always thought that was interesting since all Christians are born again. Jesus said in John 3:3, "Unless you are born again, you can never get into the Kingdom of God." Barbara understood that. She later sent me a sympathy card and indicated feeling that the lunch she had with Dad that summer was a "God-designed meeting". I believe she was right. I believe that was when it all made sense to Dad.

In a later conversation with Barbara, she told me that Dad didn't say much at all during that three-hour lunch. He was a captive audience and, during those three hours, he got to hear the truth about Jesus and the path to salvation. Just as I didn't get it from church, I don't believe Dad got it either. He was confused and I believe he thought that going to church and living a good life would get him to Heaven. But he must have learned that day that no amount of good works could get him there. No one else could forgive him of his sin and make him right before God. Only Christ. John 14:6 tells us that Jesus is the Way, the Truth, and the Life. No one comes to the Father but through Him. I know that Dad figured that out because that is the only way he could be in Heaven. I know that he is in Heaven because God told me that he is.

I recalled that after returning from that trip, Dad no longer left the room when Mom and I talked about faith. I had even mentioned it to the women in my Bible study. Dad never told me that anything had changed, but clearly something had. Although I didn't recognize it at the time, I now believed that Dad became more comfortable around discussions of faith because he finally understood that faith. I will never know for certain in this life when Dad accepted Christ. All that really matters is that he did. I looked forward to sharing that information with Mom.

Robert took the day off from school to drive me to the hospital and I was so grateful. I was still an emotional wreck and in no condition to drive. It also allowed me the opportunity to read my Bible on the way. God led me to Ephesians 3:14-16.

When I think of the wisdom and scope of His plan I fall down on my knees and pray to the Father of all the great family of God—some of them already in Heaven and some down here on earth—that out of His glorious, unlimited resources He will give you the mighty inner strengthening of His Holy Spirit.

Once again, the tears flowed in gratitude. God had given me exactly the message of encouragement I needed right then. I felt myself being filled with His strength at that very moment and I was ready to face whatever was in store for me.

I prepared myself for the worst and was relieved when Mom did not look nearly as bad as I had expected. Although she was quite swollen and hooked up to numerous tubes and monitors, she was still very recognizable. I went straight to her bedside and touched her hand. I saw her wedding ring on her swollen finger and tears filled my eyes. I didn't know if she knew about Dad. I knew that she would miss him, but I was glad that once she woke up, I could assure her that she would see him again.

I leaned over and kissed her cheek. I whispered in her ear, "I'm here, Mom. You're going to be OK." I was in complete shock when she opened her eyes! We thought she was going to be unconscious for a couple of days. The nurse explained that she was unconscious only due to the sedation. She had turned it down so Mom could wake up while we were there.

I was surprised and glad to be able to make a connection with her this soon. But she just stared at the ceiling. I talked to her and tried to get her to focus on me. It took some time, but she finally looked at me. Although she couldn't respond to me at all, I felt certain that she was going to make a full recovery.

I looked at the dry erase board on the wall in Mom's room and read the date.

December 15th, 2009

It was her birthday. That was one of the reasons that she and Dad were coming to Falls City. We had planned to celebrate it together. I thought about how we go through life making our plans, trying to be in control of things. But in one instant, everything can change. What once seemed important, no longer matters. Proverbs 16:1 says, "We can make our plans, but the final outcome is in God's hands."

I knew that was true and I was glad that I had chosen to place my life in His hand. Because I had, God had been able to prepare me for this time. He told me to quit my job so I wouldn't have that to worry about and could stay at the hospital with Mom. He strengthened my relationship with Robert so that our marriage could withstand the stress that this event would cause. And he provided for my every need during Mom's hospital stay.

There were respite rooms in the hospital for family members of patients. I spent most nights in one of those rooms and had plenty of other offers for places to stay. God even led me to an amazing Christian woman in the ICU waiting room. Nora's husband had been in a car accident ten days earlier. She offered me the extra bed in her room one night when no other rooms were available.

God continually answered my prayers and made His presence known in incredible ways. But the most amazing way was in a text message:

If u need
anything
let me
know. God

You can only imagine what I felt when I saw that message on the screen of my phone. I don't text, so I didn't really know how to read text messages. Once I figured out how to scroll down, I was able to read the remainder of the message.

bless . . . .
tyrone

Tyrone is my brother-in-law. He'd heard about the accident and wanted to offer his support. God had used his text message to communicate to me that He was there and that He would provide for my needs. I know that it wasn't coincidence that the spacing resulted in the message being displayed in that way. That was God.

CHAPTER 15

"This is why"

Through tragedy, God can bring good. I was given numerous opportunities to share my faith while Mom was in the hospital. Just a couple of days after the accident, I had dinner with two former coworkers. I took my Bible with me.

I knew that one of them struggled with faith. I had witnessed to her many times when we worked together and was glad for the opportunity to do so again. When she saw me, she expressed her surprise at my unexpected demeanor and commented, "I can't believe you're so calm."

I held up my Bible and said, "This is why."

I shared with her and Alice the agony that I felt when I heard about the accident and my fear that I would never see my father again. I told them that I prayed to God to tell me where Dad was and that He answered. I showed them the passage in Isaiah assuring me that I would see him again. I also told them about the vision.

They listened in amazement and disbelief as I told them about what God had shown me more than a month before the accident. I explained that God could show us the future because He is eternal. He knows the future because He has been there. I finally understood that God is the only One who can give us a glimpse of the future. He is the only

One with access to it. If anyone else tries to predict the future, they are either guessing or calling on evil forces to do it.

When I was in college, one of my psychology professors brought in a psychic. I don't recall why and I wish that she hadn't done so because, like so many of my other experiences before becoming a Christian, it messed me up.

After telling us about her "powers", the psychic offered to read auras and palms for the students. I was skeptical and decided to test her. I had just had a laparoscopy with a biopsy days before, but had not yet received a diagnosis. I had her read my aura and asked her if I had endometriosis. She told me that I did not have the disease, but that my pelvic organs looked "raw".

I was intrigued and thought that maybe she did have a "gift", so I had her read my palm. I asked her if I would marry and how many children I would have. She told me that I would marry twice and that my first husband would be someone that I already knew. She said that I would have three children, two boys and a girl.

Soon after that, I was told that I did indeed have endometriosis. Although the diagnosis negated the psychic's aura reading, for some reason I still believed the palm reading. I still believed that I would marry twice and have three children. I believed it even more when it turned out that she was correct in the prediction that I would marry someone I already knew. Robert and I were friends at the time of the reading. A few years later, we had two boys and one girl.

Since those predictions had come true, I feared that the psychic's other prediction would come true. If I were to marry twice, that meant that we were going to divorce or Robert was going to die. Therefore I wouldn't allow myself to get close to him. I prepared to lose him.

When I discovered that I was pregnant with Kiri, I was so excited. I believed that having a fourth child could change the future that had been predicted. If we had four children, maybe it would somehow negate the rest of the prediction of marrying twice. I dismissed the fact that it had already been negated when I received the endometriosis diagnosis. That's just how messed up I was.

Throughout my pregnancy with Kiri, I was scared that I would lose her. There was a time that I didn't feel her move for several hours and

I was sure that I had lost her. I shook my belly and poked at her until finally I felt her kick, probably quite irritated that I had interrupted her nap.

Even giving birth and seeing a beautiful and healthy baby only brought minimal reassurance. I continued to have difficulty bonding with her, still believing that she might die. I'm sure that was one of the reasons that I believed that the vision was showing me Kiri's death.

I let that woman's "predictions" affect my life in such a way that I could neither enjoy nor appreciate what God had given me. And not only did I believe something that was clearly not true, I also believed that I could do something to change it. That belief led to the "if onlys" that I felt after the accident. I really thought that I had some control over the events of that day and that I was somehow responsible for them.

Now I know that only God has control. Only He knows what is going to happen, when, how, and ultimately, why. Who are we to question?

In an e-mail update that I sent out to my Bible study friends, I wrote:

> God has a plan in everything. It is hard at times, but we have to trust in Him and know that He is in control. He has given me amazing strength. I feel His presence. Today as I was reading in Job, I found myself caressing my Bible. I realized that it was God caressing me. He has never left me and never will.
>
> As you pray for me, know that I am also praying for all of you. I pray that through my experience, you will all grow in your faith and come to trust in the Lord more and more.
>
> In Christ,
>
> Julia

While Mom was in the ICU, I had to be more like the mother rather than the daughter. I had to sign consent forms and make difficult decisions. The hardest one was choosing to have Dad's body cremated. It had been three days and Mom was still not able to talk, so I had to give consent. I knew that if he donated his body, it would have been cremated eventually. Cremation would also allow us more time for Mom's recovery before a service. It made sense, but I sure wish that I could have talked to Mom about it.

God stayed with me through all of the trials and comforted me along the way with His Word. He led me to the eighth chapter of Romans. In particular, I was comforted by Romans 8:28, which is my favorite verse and was already highlighted.

And we know that all that happens to us is working for our good if we love God and are fitting into His plans.

Although this has been my favorite verse for a long time, I have never been able to memorize it word for word because I've read it in so many different translations. This is from The Living Bible, which is the one Jeff gave me.

I thought about Jeff and how he obeyed God by reaching out to me, but never saw me come to salvation. That's how it is for many Christians. We follow God's lead, but often we don't get to see the outcome of our obedience; at least not in this life. One day I will see Jeff again in Heaven and will have the opportunity to thank him. I look forward to introducing him to my father.

Like Jeff, I had finally learned to follow God's lead. After going home overnight to see Sheila's Christmas program, I was gathering things to return to Lincoln. As I picked up my purse, I felt compelled to take some salvation prayer cards out of my Bible case and place them in the outside pocket of my purse. I didn't know why, but I've learned that when I feel compelled to do something, I need to do it.

At suppertime that evening, I went to Taco John's. I wasn't sure why I wasn't just eating in the hospital cafeteria, but something, or Someone, was leading me to Taco John's. So I went. As I placed my order, I felt my heart racing and experienced a sense of tension for no apparent reason. I opened my purse to pay and one of the salvation prayer cards fell out onto the counter. I knew that God was telling me that I needed to witness to the cashier.

I asked him, "Are you a Christian?"

He replied, "No. I'm an atheist."

I said, "God sent me here to talk to you," as I led him to a table.

I had brought my Bible in with me, which was not something that I would ever typically do, but then I understood why. I told him about my parents' accident and showed him the verse in Isaiah assuring me of my dad's salvation. I told him that God is real and that He speaks to us through His Word.

God had already been working on this young man. After listening to me for several minutes, Chad told me that someone else had visited him a few days ago and told him many of the same things about God's love and Christ's offer of salvation. But as I talked to him, he kept looking over my shoulder. I truly believe that a demon was standing right behind me. I continued to share with him how much God loved him and wanted to offer him eternal life, but he pulled away and went back to work.

I prayed for him and felt God telling me to write a note on the back of my receipt. I wrote:

Chad,

By the end of tonight, there will be over 1000 people praying for you. Your parents love you and so does He.

I wasn't sure why I had written those words except that I felt God telling me to do so. I gave the note to another cashier and asked him to give it to Chad. I wrote about him in my e-mail that night.

Tonight God led me to witness to the cashier at Taco John's. His name is Chad and he told me that he was an atheist. He listened as I shared with him, but then pulled away. God told me to write him a note telling him that by the end of tonight, there would be over 1000 people praying for him. So please pray and forward this e-mail on to others who will pray also.

Through the suffering and pain of losing my father, I was given opportunities to reach out to my coworker and to Chad. I prayed that each of them might see God through my experience and choose to place their lives in His hand as I had. I prayed that they would accept Christ and be saved.

In my Bible time before bed, God led me to Ephesians 1:8-10.

And he has showered down upon us the richness of his grace—for how well he understands us and knows what is best for us at all times. God has told us His secret reason for sending Christ, a plan He decided on in mercy long ago; and this was His purpose: that when the time is ripe He will gather us all together from wherever we are—in heaven or on earth—to be with Him in Christ, forever.

God does know what is best for us—all of us. He knew that we would sin and be separated from Him and would need a Savior. He sent His Son to be that Savior. Because of His sacrifice, one day those who believe in Him will all be together, those who have already died and those who are still here.

God also showed me Romans 8:38, "For I am convinced that nothing can ever separate us from his love. Death can't, and life can't." I knew that Dad was with God and nothing could separate him from God's love. For those of us who know Him, we can be assured of the same.

CHAPTER 16

His *presence*

The Sunday morning after the accident, I woke up feeling on the verge of tears. I even put on waterproof mascara because I felt that the tears would flow at any moment. I went to church and when I read the topic of the sermon, I understood why I had felt so teary.

"Tears"

Pastor Tim spoke on the shortest verse in the Bible: John 11:35, "Jesus wept." (NIV) He talked about how Jesus weeps with us when we are hurting. I was so glad that I had put on the waterproof mascara because the tears were streaming down my cheeks throughout his message. I knew that Jesus was crying with me and that was comforting. It also gave me permission to cry. I had not done much of that yet and really needed to.

Pastor Tim also talked about the time when there will be no more tears. Revelation 21:4 tells us, "He will wipe away all tears from their eyes, and there shall be no more death, nor sorrow, nor crying, nor pain. All of that has gone forever." I look forward to that day and knowing that it will come enables me to live in peace now.

In addition to the topic of tears, Pastor Tim also talked about Christmas. He said that it's not about "presents" like so many people have made it to be. Instead it's about God's "presence" among us. That really spoke to me as I remembered how I had chosen to go to church on Christmas Eve just to get to open a present after the service. I really did believe that Christmas was just all about giving and receiving presents. I didn't understand the true reason for it. Since I have come to understand the truth, I've been really bothered by how commercialized this sacred holiday has become. There's so much talk about gift giving on Christmas, that the true reason for the Holy Day often gets lost.

Pastor Tim's sermon also made me think about how I had tried the previous year to change a long-standing family tradition of exchanging presents for Christmas. I suggested that instead of buying gifts, we take the money we would have spent and give it to a Christian charity. But I approached it in the wrong way. I tried to get others to change and they weren't ready to do so.

When I sought God's guidance in His Word, He led me to the story of Shadrach, Meshach, and Abednego. He was telling me to stand up for what I believed in, what I knew to be right. But I didn't, because standing alone was hard. Robert and I gave in and carried on the tradition that year. I regretted that decision. I now understand that God does not ask us to do things that are easy or popular. He asks us to do what is right. Jesus says in Luke 14:27 that no one can be His disciple unless he carries his own cross and follows Him.

This year as Christmas approached, I felt a great deal of anxiety, knowing that we would once again be expected to purchase and accept gifts when we knew that that was not what Christmas was meant to be about. I felt compelled to revisit the idea of giving to charity. Robert suggested that instead of trying to change others, we should start with our immediate family. We sent a list of charities to the family members who had our names for the gift exchange and asked for donations to be sent to them in our names. We felt good about that decision and knew that we were impacting the next generation.

I knew that her family's presence would mean far more to Mom than any presents we could give her this year. Robert and I decided that he and the kids would come to Lincoln to be with Grandma on Christmas. But a snowstorm was predicted and in order to get them to Lincoln before the storm, it would mean four nights in a motel at a cost of nearly $400. Robert was concerned that we couldn't afford it. I said, "God will provide," but I had no idea how. Then I looked at my phone messages. Some friends of my parents had called earlier that evening and left this message:

Call if there is anything we can do.
Tom and Margo

I called Margo and before I even mentioned that Robert and the kids were coming to Lincoln, she said, "I don't know why I didn't mention this before, but we own a condo there in Lincoln and we would love for you to use it."

I sat in amazement. God provided just as I knew He would.

In my e-mail that night, I wrote:

Today I have been reminded of the song, "Blessed Be Your Name". The lyrics say, "He gives and takes away, my heart will always say, blessed be Your name." When I told the kids of Grandpa's death, Justin (our 11-year-old) said, "God gives and God takes away." What an amazing response for an 11-year-old! Already he understands that everything we have is a gift from God. God gives to us and He takes from us. But through it all, we are to praise Him.

As we approach Christmas, I hope that we can all remember the true gift of Christmas was not a *present*, but God's *presence*. Many of you will celebrate the holiday by exchanging presents wrapped in pretty paper. But let us not forget that God's gift was a tiny baby wrapped in cloths. And nothing in this world can compare to that gift.

The next day, Mom was really uncomfortable. I missed breakfast and supper because I didn't want to leave her. The stress and lack of food resulted in a migraine. The short times that I was able to leave her, I spent lying down in the respite room trying to relax away the headache.

Mom's pastor visited that day. He read to her from Philippians 4. I looked it up later and found that verses 6-7 and 12-13 were highlighted in my Bible.

Don't worry about anything; instead pray about everything; tell God your needs and don't forget to thank Him for His answers. If you do this you will experience God's peace, which is far more wonderful than the human mind can understand . . . I have learned the secret of contentment in every situation, whether it be a full stomach or hunger, plenty or want; for I can do everything God asks me to with the help of Christ who gives me the strength and power.

In spite of my hunger and pain that day, I was able to be there for Mom with the almighty strength of the Holy Spirit. As I drifted off to sleep that night, I was reminded of Lamentations 3:23, "Great is His faithfulness; His loving kindness begins afresh each day."

CHAPTER 17

Take your time and pray

On December 23rd, Mom was moved to the rehabilitation unit. Nine days after the accident and only one day after surgery to repair her broken jaw, she was ready for rehabilitation. The power of prayer is phenomenal and I knew that she could not have progressed as quickly as she had without it.

I read many get well cards to Mom that day. One had a verse that is dear to my heart. 1 Peter 5:7 "Cast all your anxiety upon Him because He cares for you." (NIV) My translation says, "Let him have all your worries and cares, for He is always thinking about you and watching everything that concerns you."

I reflected upon those words. I had no worries throughout this ordeal because I knew that God was watching over us. He was in control and I could rest in that knowledge. I thought of the many people who were brought into the hospital due to accidents and I wondered how many of them were trying to deal with the tragedies without God's strength. I knew that I could not possibly get through this without Him and was glad that I had made the choice to be in His hand.

When we arrived at the condo on Christmas Eve, Randal said that he wanted to be home for Christmas rather than where we were. Robert reminded him that Mary and Joseph spent the first Christmas away from their home, too. They had to travel to Bethlehem. God leads us where we need to be, which might not be where we want to be. It wasn't ideal, but at least we were together. And as my mother taught me, that is really what matters on Christmas—and throughout the year.

After the kids went to bed, Robert and I filled Christmas stockings with some small gifts and placed them under the fireplace. It wasn't the kind of Christmas we were planning, but I was glad that we were not participating in a huge gift exchange. I was relieved to get away from the commercialization of this sacred holiday. I thought of all of the people in this world who spend hundreds of dollars every year on presents for one another and don't understand the true meaning of Christmas. They don't know who Jesus is and why He came. I prayed for them that they, like me, would come to an understanding and accept the only gift that has ever really mattered on Christmas—the gift of salvation that Jesus offers through His sacrifice.

Not only do we receive the gift of salvation when we accept Christ, we also receive the Holy Spirit. Ephesians 1:14 tells us that His presence within us is God's guarantee that He really will give us all that He promised. In 1 Corinthians 10:13, God promises that He will provide us a way out of temptation and one day in the hospital cafeteria, I was thankful for that promise.

I had gone to the cafeteria for lunch as I did every day. My "usual" table was taken, so I sat near the wall facing the entry. I was feeling incredibly alone. Those are often the times when Satan attacks. I looked around the cafeteria and my eyes were drawn to an attractive man. I found myself looking at his hand to see if he was wearing a wedding ring. I realized what I was doing and immediately looked down. I whispered, "Satan, you are not going to do this to me."

I kept my eyes down and forced myself not to look up, until I felt compelled to do so. My eyes met the gaze of an older woman. Somehow I knew that I knew her, but I didn't know how. She approached me and asked, "Are you Julie?"

I was known as Julie when I was a child and that was when she knew me. She had worked at my elementary school. She and her friend had come to visit Mom. I invited them to join me and shared with them how God had been taking care of Mom and me through this experience. I thanked the Holy Spirit for taking care of me just then.

After they left, I called Robert. I asked him, "Do you remember that scene in 'Fireproof' when Catherine was in the hospital cafeteria?"

He asked, "Do you mean the one with the doctor hitting on her or the one with the old lady?"

I said, "Both."

I told him about my experience in the cafeteria of being tempted by Satan and then rescued by God. He was appreciative that I chose to share that with him.

I thought more about the movie. In "Fireproof", Catherine struggled with trying to care for her mother who had suffered a stroke and had lost the ability to speak. I really identified with her character. Mom had been my confidant. Whenever I was struggling in my marriage, or with anything, I would talk to her. Even though she might not have always given the best advice, just talking it out would help.

While Mom was in the ICU, she was completely unable to speak, so I just talked to her. I told her how sorry I was for being so defiant as a teenager. To this day, I am amazed that both of us survived my adolescence. Mom did the best that she knew how, but as she has often said, no one is ever truly prepared to be a parent.

Mom tried to make up for some of her mistakes as a parent by becoming a mentor. I really admired her for that and told her so. I thanked her for the lessons that she did teach me and apologized for not appreciating them at the time. I thanked her for making me strong and bold, characteristics that I cherish and have helped me in many ways. I thanked her for sharing her knowledge of nursing with me so that I knew what some of those numbers on the monitors meant and I knew something about the medications they were giving her.

I was really grateful for that time that Mom couldn't talk because it gave me the opportunity to just talk to her without concern for how she would respond. She doesn't remember most of what happened when she was in the hospital or any of what I said to her. I'm really glad that I was taking notes for this book so that she can now read about how God took care of her and me.

Christmas day I wondered if we would even get to see Mom. It had been snowing for some time and none of the side streets had been cleared. I was so glad that Robert was there with his Ford Escape. He is an excellent driver and was able to maneuver through the drifts and get us safely to the hospital. The two snowplows that we followed much of the way there really helped, too.

Mom was surprised to see us considering the weather. We hung out with her for most of the day just watching TV and playing games. We had our Christmas dinner in the hospital cafeteria. It was nothing like I was planning to prepare at home, but at least I didn't have to make it or clean up.

As I was eating my roast turkey and mashed potatoes, I thought about Dad and how he was spending Christmas with Jesus Himself. I missed Dad, but I knew that he wouldn't want to be anywhere else. Who would?

I didn't want to see the car. I knew that it would be really hard. But Mom's luggage was in it and she needed clothes in the rehab unit. I asked Robert to come with me. I knew that I would need his help digging out the luggage and getting the license plates off, but mostly I knew that I needed the emotional support.

We had to trudge through deep snow to even get to the car. Once we reached it, I couldn't believe what I saw. The passenger side of the car was completely smashed in. It was obvious that there was no way that Dad could have survived that impact. I looked in the passenger window and suddenly recalled the scene from my vision. It was the empty seat! The "debris" I had seen was snow.

The past Sunday in church the sermon was on sacrifice. I couldn't help but consider the sacrifice my father had made. After the accident, Robert said that Dad had fulfilled his God-given responsibility as a husband. He protected his wife and died for her. I know that he was proud of having done so. And although I miss him terribly, I'm proud of him too. I believed that if he had to choose how he was going to die, that would have been his choice.

When I got back to Lincoln and was near the hospital, a song came on the radio that caught my attention. I had never heard it before, but I felt as though Dad was speaking to Mom and me through it. It is called, "The Words I Would Say" by Sidewalk Prophets. Here's the final chorus:

Be strong in the Lord and never give up hope.
You're gonna do great things, I already know.
God's got His hand on you so don't live life in fear.
Forgive and forget, but don't forget why you're here,
Take your time and pray, thank God for each day,
His love will find a way. These are the words I would say.

I was overwhelmed with awe at how God continued to give me just what I needed just when I needed it. That song gave me such comfort and the determination I needed to carry on. And it reminded me that the most important thing I could do now, or at any time, is to take my time and pray.

CHAPTER 18

God is in control

I woke up on January 1st, 2010 wondering what this new year might bring. We had not talked yet about where Mom might live. We knew that she would be coming to our home to recover, but then what? I knew that she wanted to go back to Holdrege, but I hated the idea of her living in such a big house all alone. There would be so many memories of Dad. I couldn't see how she could bear it. I really hoped that she might consider moving to Falls City to be closer to us.

I recalled a few months earlier when I was talking with her about taking Kayelee back into our home. I told her that I was worried that having five kids would be more than I could handle. Mom suggested the possibility of her and Dad moving to Falls City to help us out. But after talking it over with him, they decided not to because Dad was involved in so many things in Holdrege and played piano at a restaurant in a nearby city. I began to wonder if God had laid that desire on her heart knowing that when the time came to actually move, Dad would no longer be with her.

That day we talked about how God had prepared us for these events. Mom found the very house where she would be spending her recovery. Her persistence in wanting to see it resulted in us buying that house. It even has a guest room on the main floor with an attached bathroom. I wish I could recall the exact words Mom said at that point. It was something to the effect of, "It would probably be a whole lot easier if we would just all accept that God is in control and we are not."

I was surprised to hear her say something like that considering that she had always wanted to be in control of everything. She's learned a lot from this experience and her faith has grown in ways I could not have ever even imagined. I'm glad to have been a part of it and I know that Dad is pleased.

I wrote in an e-mail message:

> It has been quite an emotional roller coaster for all of us. But we know that we are not alone on it. God is with us through all of the ups and downs, twists and turns. And through it all, He remains in control. As long as we trust in Him, we know that we can get through anything.
>
> Many people have told me that they are amazed at how strong I have been through this and I tell them that it is solely because of my faith. Without it, I would be a wreck. I know that God is in control and He has a plan. In the wake of tragedy, He will bring about something beautiful.

I received a very encouraging response the next day.

> Julia,
>
> I am not at all surprised at how well you are coping. Your dad always said you were the strong one . . . I worked with him at the paper for many years. We were all talking about what we accomplished in our lives and what we wanted to, his answer was "my girls". And, you know, who could top that? . . .
>
> Lauri

One of the things that I really appreciated about Dad was that he believed in us—all of us. He never gave up on my sisters when others did and I know that his encouragement allowed them to achieve far more than they could have without it. He also never gave up on me even when I doubted myself. He gave me the courage to carry on when it would have been so much easier to just give up. Whenever I considered dropping out of college, I recalled his words, "You can do anything you set your mind to." Even while writing this book, I felt him spurring me on to finish.

Dad was a writer. He worked for the local newspaper for many years. I loved reading his column, "The Roving Maniac". He called it that because his home state was Maine and people from there are often referred to as "Maniacs". His writing was thoughtful, humorous, and captivating.

In sixth grade, my best friend, Holly, and I would walk to his office to have lunch with Dad. He was always happy to see us. I would sit at his desk and read what he had been writing. I think that is when I began to develop an interest in writing. I never really pursued it though, until now.

Mom was discharged from the hospital on Monday, January 4, 2010, less than three weeks after the accident. I couldn't believe the amazing recovery. It truly was a miracle.

But when we arrived home, things were not as I had hoped. Many of the tasks that I had asked to be done while I was gone were not. I immediately became angry. All of the bitterness and resentment that I had left behind while at the hospital returned.

The next evening, while I was preparing supper, Mom went to sit in the chair and fell. Although there was nothing they could have done, I blamed Robert and the kids because they were in the same room. I also blamed myself. I wondered if she was really ready to be home. I felt completely overwhelmed and incapable.

That night I couldn't sleep. At 1:45 AM I went to the computer and typed out my frustration:

> I really thought that getting home would be easier, but it comes with all of its own set of challenges. First, there is settling in

and establishing a routine. With a preschool daughter and a frail mother, it is nearly impossible to get anything done. I can't do anything without leaving them out of my sight. Mom took a fall off a chair tonight. She is not really hurt, but what is next? I am beginning to wonder if this is more than I can handle.

I am sorry to say that Robert and the kids provide only minimal help, which exacerbates the situation. Just providing Mom the physical care and nutrition is a full time job. Then we add a husband and four kids, and a large house to keep organized and I am over the top. And before you know it, we will have to plan a memorial service.

I know that God is at work through this ordeal, I just sometimes wonder if He picked the wrong one.

God responded through one of His children. In response to my desperate cry, Leslie sent me this scripture passage, message of encouragement, and prayer from Joel Osteen:

> "This is my command—be strong and courageous! Do not be afraid or discouraged. For the Lord your God is with you wherever you go." (Joshua 1:9, NLT)
>
> Remember, the power that is in you is greater than the power of fear. When thoughts come that say, "You're not able", choose faith by saying, "I can do all things through Christ!" Choose faith today so you can overcome fear and live in the freedom God has in store for you!
>
> "Heavenly Father, I receive Your Word today which is life, health, and strength to me. I choose to close the door on fear by guarding what I say, what I listen to, and what I dwell on . . . Fill me with Your love and faith, and I meditate on Your Word. In Jesus' Name. Amen."
>
> "Be strong and courageous." It seems so simple—and it should be. What do we have to fear? Has not God shown His presence,

His power, His control all along? What should make me think that He would abandon me now?

I had to ask myself that question. What should make me think that He would abandon me now? He certainly has shown His presence, His power, and His control. Just the fact that Mom was out of the hospital so soon was evidence of His power. My incredible sense of peace for so long was evidence of His presence. And all of the events that led up to this were evidence of His control. How could I possibly doubt His presence now?

I didn't. I knew that He was still there. Like every other time in my life when I didn't feel Him, it was me who was pulling away. I was trying to handle things on my own rather than continuing to rely on Him. And when I try to do things on my own, I always mess it up. So I put myself back in His hand.

CHAPTER 19

Save a place for me

Because there was no Christian radio in Falls City, I relied on my CDs. I listened to my Matthew West CD and heard his song, "Save a Place for Me". Although I had heard the song before, I had never really paid attention to the lyrics. But this time I did. It begins like this:

Don't be mad if I cry, it just hurts so bad sometimes
'Cause everyday it's sinking in and I have to say goodbye all over again
You know I bet it feels good to have the weight of this world off your shoulders now
I'm dreaming of the day when I'm finally there with you
Save a place for me, save a place for me
I'll be there soon, I'll be there soon

The tears flowed as I listened to that song for what seemed like the first time. As I listened, I imagined Dad in Heaven, free from the cares of this world, waiting for me, and saving a place for me. Later in the song, Matthew West says, "I'll pray, with every tear, and be thankful for the time I had you here." I am so thankful for the time that Dad was here and I learned that many others were thankful for him also.

After Mom decided to move to Falls City to be closer to family, we had a memorial service for Dad in Holdrege. When we entered the sanctuary, we were amazed to see the many people whose lives had been touched by Dad.

"Amazing Grace" was Dad's favorite hymn and it was being sung as we walked in. The same song was sung at my grandmother's funeral. It was her favorite also. I had a sense that she was with Dad and they were looking down on us together.

I delivered the eulogy. I worked on it for two days, hoping to honor Dad for who he was. God helped me to express it just right:

> I was lying awake the other night thinking about this service today. I was thinking about what I would want to say about Dad when 1 Corinthians 13:4-8 on the characteristics of love came to mind.
>
> *Love is very patient and kind, never jealous or envious, never boastful or proud, never haughty or selfish or rude. Love does not demand its own way. It is not irritable or touchy. It does not hold grudges and will hardly even notice when others do it wrong. It is never glad about injustice, but rejoices whenever truth wins out. If you love someone you will be loyal to him no matter what the cost. You will always believe in him, always expect the best of him, and always stand your ground in defending him. All the special gifts and powers from God will someday come to an end, but love goes on forever.*
>
> Dad was always patient and kind. He always had time for others no matter how busy he might be. He was never selfish or rude. He would put others' needs ahead of his own any day. He certainly never demanded his own way. In fact, he was very quiet and reserved and would never argue with anyone. He never held a grudge, but was quick to forgive and forget. He was loyal and would stick by his family no matter what. Dad believed in all of us and that gave me the courage to carry on even when things got tough. He exemplified love.
>
> He demonstrated the sacrificial love of Christ every day of his life and even in his death. I am sorry to say that I did not recognize that as I should have while he was still with us. I often took him for granted and I regret that terribly.

In my growing up years and even as an adult, Dad taught me so many valuable life lessons that I am just now beginning to learn. He was never pushy in his teaching. He led by example. And I hope to follow that example more.

One thing that bothered me about Dad was that he was never verbal about his faith. But looking back on his life, he clearly lived it out. He didn't talk the talk, but he did walk the walk. And I am so proud of him for that and I truly hope to honor him by walking that walk just like he did.

I love you, Daddy. And I can't wait to see you again. Save a place for me.

I walked back to my seat and knew that Dad was pleased. That was enough for me.

After the service, I invited anyone who wished to share memories of Dad to do so. Right away many people came up or raised their hands. The stories were incredible. Dad had given of himself in more ways than I even knew.

Bob told of Dad insisting on driving him to Kearney for surgery and spending over thirty minutes in the pharmacy waiting for his prescription. Tuney told of Dad offering him a place to stay after a house fire.

I learned that Dad had been involved in Vacation Bible School at the church. He played Paul in a skit and really impacted a four-year-old boy who came to the service.

Dad was also a mentor for TeamMates. His mentee, Dylan, was there. He read a letter he had composed after learning of Dad's death.

Hi, my name is Dylan . . . and I want to tell you about my friend Jack. When I was in 5th grade they started the mentor program in my school and I was so excited to get a mentor and his name is Jack. Jack would come to school once a week and eat lunch with me, and we would play games or just talk. Jack and I decided one day we liked reading and playing games more than playing in the gym, cause as Jack says he is not gym material, and you know I'm not either. We had so much fun together. We were in the Swedish Days parade riding on a float and did so many other fun things together like making crafts. I

looked forward to each time Jack would come to school and spend time with me. Jack I love you a lot! I know you're in heaven singing and playing the piano for God. Jack you will always have a special place in my heart. Your friend always,
Dylan

Nearly everyone in the room was in tears after that. Dad touched so many lives in the time he was here and I know he will continue to do so long after his death.

Kiri took the mic next. She said, "Grandpa was in an accident and went to the 'hostible'. Then he got better and went home."

I thought that she was still confused and did not realize that Grandpa had died. But later I concluded that she was not confused at all. She knew that Grandpa is at home. During the service, the pastor talked about Jesus preparing a place for us in Heaven. Dad was in his place, prepared just for him.

CHAPTER 20

Safe in His hand

When Mom moved to Falls City, she started attending NorthRidge Church with us and it made a huge difference in her faith walk. I didn't fully understand the impact until one week when she joined us in our Sunday School class. As an introduction, we were asked to say our names and then identify the person who has had the greatest spiritual influence in our life. Mom identified me. She thanked me for all that I had taught her and especially for bringing her to NorthRidge Church.

Although I miss my father, I know that many good things have happened as a result of his death. Mom had opportunities to grow in her faith that she had not previously experienced. Many other people also grew in their faith while watching us relying on God through our ordeal. Our perspectives shifted to the eternal rather than the here and now. When I looked back on Dad's life, I saw that he was already doing that. He stored up his treasures in Heaven, where he is enjoying them now. I know that he wants us to do the same.

After Mom decided to move, I was lying awake in bed wondering if it was the right decision. So I did what I often do when I am uncertain about something. I went to my Bible and, as always, I found the comfort and peace I was looking for. God led me to the 35th chapter of Isaiah, which tells about God's final Kingdom. I realized that it really doesn't matter where we live on this earth, because this is not our final home. Our home is with God.

Kayelee moved back into our home in March. Although we indicated a willingness to make a long-term commitment to her, we didn't feel that God intended for her to stay with us. We told her that we would keep her until He laid it on our hearts to adopt her or until He revealed another family to do so. She seemed at peace with the assurance that she was safe in God's hand.

In April, we had the second memorial service with Dad's family. My aunts and cousins flew in from all over the country. The last time we were all together was when Grandma died four years ago. Since that time, I had grown tremendously in my faith and felt led to use the eulogy as an opportunity to share that faith with my extended family. This is what I wrote:

It's hard to believe that his death was nearly four months ago because I feel the loss of my father just as strongly today as I did then. He is and always will be deeply missed by many. It wasn't until after his death that I learned just how many lives my father had touched and how truly missed he would be. I knew that Dad was amazingly generous. If anyone was in need of anything and Dad had it to give, there was no hesitation. He would give it. I knew that he was incredibly loyal—to his family, his work, his church, and his community. He would never turn his back on anyone no matter the cost. Dad was a good person.

Yet I knew that no matter how much good he did, he couldn't earn a place in Heaven. Romans 3:23 tells us that we *all* have sinned and fall short of the glory of God. Verse 27 tells us that our salvation is not based on our good deeds, but on what Christ has done and our faith in Him. But Dad never liked to talk about faith or salvation so I didn't have that absolute certainty that I would see him again and that tore me apart.

So that night I prayed and I asked God to let me know for certain where Dad was. And He did. God led me to the book of Isaiah chapter 57. As I opened my Bible, right at the top of the page, I read the heading, "The godly shall rest in peace." Tears of joy and gratitude fell down my face as I read the first two verses. (I read Isaiah 57:1-2) As hard as it was to accept that he was gone, I could rest in the assurance that I would one day see him again.

In the days and weeks after that, I began hearing stories from others whose lives Dad had touched and I was truly amazed. I realized that I didn't even really know my father like I thought I did. I heard stories of him going out of his way to help others, neither asking nor expecting anything in return. He gave more than I ever knew whether it be his time, his resources, or his talents. He acted in an incredibly loving way even toward those whom others might consider unlovable. He was even involved in Vacation Bible School playing the part of Paul in a skit. I had no idea because Dad didn't do those things for recognition or praise. He did them because he was filled with the Holy Spirit.

Reading that passage in Isaiah told me that Dad accepted the gift of salvation offered to us through Christ's sacrifice, the sacrifice that we celebrated just over a week ago (on Good Friday) and *that* assured him of his place in Heaven. His good deeds didn't save him. They couldn't, only faith in Christ can. But in the book of James, we learn that faith is dead if it does not result in good works. Dad's faith was alive and it resulted in numerous good works. And so I realized that Dad didn't need to say that he was a Christian because he lived as a Christian. He demonstrated his faith through action, and actions truly do speak louder than words.

1 Peter 5:5-6 says that God gives special blessings to those who are humble and in His good time, He will lift them up. Dad was humble and God lifted him up. And he is now enjoying those blessings. In The Message that passage reads, "God has had it with the proud, but takes delight in just plain people, so be content with who you are, and don't put on airs." A friend of the family described Dad by saying that he just seemed "comfortable in his own skin". He certainly was. He never tried to be someone that he wasn't.

So now my only regret is that I didn't appreciate Dad more or even recognize all that he was doing when he was here and I didn't honor him for it. So I hope to do that now by living my life more like he did.

I love you, Daddy, and I miss you. But I know that I am going to see you again and I look forward to that day. So save a place for me. I'll be there soon.

After I delivered the eulogy, we showed a slideshow of pictures of Dad with the Matthew West song, "Save a Place for Me" playing. Randal did an awesome job putting it together. It was incredibly moving and many were in tears, including me. I prayed that the words in my eulogy or the words in the song would touch the hearts of those listening.

We honored Dad through music in the rest of the service. Justin played his saxophone, Randal played the drums, and Levi played the piano. My cousin, Katie, played the flute while Sheila and Kayelee sang "Amazing Grace". I prayed that those lyrics would also speak to those in attendance. I hoped that Dad's death would result in others receiving eternal life by recognizing their need for a Savior as he did.

We also honored Dad at the luncheon after the service by ordering pizza. Dad always hated when we made a fuss over special dinners. He would often say, "Why don't we just order pizza?"

Less than a year after the accident, Chuck and Julie moved away. Like us, they follow God wherever He leads them. But before they left, they got the ball rolling to bring NorthRidge Church to Falls City.

On August 22, 2010, we had our first service at NorthRidge Nebraska. We met in a storefront in downtown Falls City. The first item we had written in the margin in the *Experiencing God* book had been fulfilled. We now had an "Evangelical church in Falls City". And the second item, "Minister to Kayelee," resulted in a new family being identified for her.

Mike and Heather also attended NorthRidge. We got to know them after we began bringing Kayelee to the church. It didn't take long before we felt God telling us that they were the parents He had chosen for her. Heather said that she had felt for some time that their family was not complete. Kayelee moved in with them right after Tim and Jill made the difficult and loving decision to relinquish their parental rights. All three of the children finally had new families.

As I am writing the final chapter of this book, our family is beginning a new chapter in our lives. Soon after the last child was placed and the church had been started, God made it clear to us that our purposes for being led to Falls City had been accomplished and it was time to go. Robert resigned as Falls City band director and we once again placed our lives fully in God's hand to lead us.

Again we endured several months of uncertainty before feeling His lead. He led us back to Lincoln, right back into our old house. But, as is often the case, I found myself questioning. I didn't understand why He would take us away when we were accomplishing so much in Falls City. And I certainly didn't know why He would bring us back to where we had already been. Remember, when we question God, He answers.

More than a week after moving, I drove back to our house in Falls City to retrieve some items we had left. I went on a Sunday so I could go to church one last time at NorthRidge Nebraska. Our campus pastor's wife was excited to see me and handed me a sealed envelope that she had intended to mail to us in Lincoln. I thanked her and tucked it away to open later.

After the service, I went to show the house to some potential renters. As we walked around, I described all of the things we had done to the home in the past three years. They asked me if it was hard leaving it. I had to admit that it was. After they left, I looked around and continued my questioning of whether we had made the right choice in leaving. I wondered if God really had led us away.

I packed up the car and prepared to head for Lincoln, but decided to first open that envelope that Jenny had given me. It was as though God had sent me a note through her. In that envelope was a copy of a daily devotional titled "God's Mighty Hand".

You have a strong arm; Your hand is mighty, Your right hand is exalted. Psalm 89:13

God has you in His hand, and His hand is a mighty hand. Mighty not only to save and to keep, but mighty to deliver. He brought the children of Israel "out of Egypt with a mighty hand, when they cried out to Him" (Deuteronomy 9:26; Exodus 2:23-25). Can He not also deliver you with His mighty hand? [Taken from a daily calendar called "Just a moment with you, God" by Kay Arthur]

It was dated July 9th. Jenny had written in the margin, "This was your moving day." I broke down and bawled. God was assuring me that it was His hand leading us. Every bit of doubt vanished.

I received even more assurance whenever I would listen to the Christian radio station in Lincoln. I kept hearing the song "God of this City" by Chris Tomlin. The chorus says, "For greater things have yet to come and greater things are still to be done in this city."

God has a plan for us here and as long as we remain in His hand, He will fulfill that plan through us. It may not be easy and we will likely face many more trials in the process, but we are reminded of how He has taken care of us in the past. And we are reminded that all that happens to us is working for our good *because* we love God and are fitting into His plans.

CONCLUSION

Shortly before this book was published, our daughter, Sheila, was baptized. She was eight. Like Justin, she was given the opportunity to choose who would baptize her. She chose me. I felt honored, yet so unworthy. I certainly had not been a perfect example of a Christian. But only an imperfect person could have led her to Christ because we're all imperfect.

Many imperfect people tried to lead me to Christ, but I refused to follow them. Instead I chose to follow other imperfect people who led me away from Him. But I don't blame any of them for the choices I made. I don't blame my parents, my church, my peers, or even the media. I can't even blame Satan because, although I was in his hand, I could have chosen to leave at any time. Instead I refused to even acknowledge the other hand reaching out to me.

I refused to accept the reality of God until I could *see* evidence of His hand in my life. For many years, I didn't see it because I wasn't looking for it. Even when I began seeking, I still couldn't see God's hand, because I had my back turned to Him.

I've occasionally used this illustration with clients who denied God because they couldn't "see" Him. I would ask them to turn their chair around so they couldn't see me and would then ask them if I was still there. Of course, they admitted that I was even though they couldn't see me.

It's just the same with God. Once I turned around, I "saw" Him. I saw clear evidence of God's hand in my life. I saw how He had been reaching out to me all along. I saw how He had tried to protect me when I placed myself in harm's way. He was there through all of it—both the good and the bad. Like in the famous, "Footprints" poem, God was carrying me through all of the difficult times in my life. He never left me.

A few months after my parents' accident, I heard a song on the radio called, "Bring the Rain" by Mercy Me. The chorus says:

Bring me joy, bring me peace
Bring the chance to be free
Bring me anything that brings You glory
And I know there'll be days
When this life brings me pain
But if that's what it takes to praise You
Jesus, bring the rain

Those lyrics really spoke to me. I wanted only the joy and peace and refused to acknowledge God in my pain. But I now know that trials bring us closer to Him. James 1:2 says, "Consider it pure joy, my brothers, whenever you face trials of many kinds." (NIV) Those trials cause us to turn to God for strength and wisdom. We learn to rely on Him rather than on ourselves. I finally learned to do that and was then able to praise Him through some of the greatest trials of my life.

I can now praise God through both the good and the bad times because *all* of these things bring Him glory. And they all remind me that I am not in control and was never meant to be. God is in control and has been all along. He knows what is going to happen and will bring something good out of what seems so bad. He brought this book out of those "bad" experiences.

I pray that through reading this book, many people will see the hand of God, maybe for the first time. Hopefully many will come to a saving faith in Christ and choose to place their lives in God's hand. If that happens, then I know that Dad's life, and his death, served a great purpose.

If you have come to recognize God and are ready to accept the gift that He offers you through the sacrifice of His Son, you can pray a prayer like this:

Heavenly Father, thank You for loving me and revealing Yourself to me. Thank You for sending Your Son, Jesus, to die in my place, to pay the penalty for my sin, and to offer me eternal life. I choose today to accept that gift. I choose, Father God, to place my life in Your hand. Forgive me for my sins, come into my life, and make me a new creation. In Jesus' name, Amen.

If you prayed that prayer and have chosen to place your life in God's hand, welcome to the family. You are now my brother or sister in Christ and we will one day meet in Heaven, if not before. The first thing you should do now is to tell your family and friends. Don't conceal your faith. Save your loved ones the agony that I felt when my father died. Let them know that when you leave this earth, they will see you again. If they are not Christians, share your newfound faith with them and pray that they will make the same choice.

If you are already a Christian, but haven't spoken to anyone about it, let me remind you of the Great Commission. "Therefore go and make disciples in all the nations, baptizing them into the name of the Father and of the Son and of the Holy Spirit, and teach these new disciples to obey all of the commands I have given you; and be sure of this—that I am with you always, even to the end of the world." (Matthew 28: 19-20)

Jesus made it very clear. My job, and yours if you are a Christian, is to lead others to Christ. So after reading this book, don't put it on a bookshelf. Give it to someone else who might not know Christ. Share your own faith journey with them. Then pray that they will come to know Him, too.

When someone you know becomes a Christian, disciple them. Lead them along the path so that they might not stumble because, once you become a Christian, the journey doesn't end. It's just beginning.

Whether you're a new Christian or have been a believer for many years, it's important to attend a good Bible-believing church. As I mentioned earlier in this book, there is no perfect church or denomination. The most important thing to consider is whether your church teaches from a Biblical standpoint. If you are hearing anything that is contrary to the Bible, or if you are discouraged from reading the

Bible on you own, get out. Find a church that does not compromise Biblical truth for political correctness or for it's own gain.

Once you find a good church, get involved. Join small groups and fellowship with other Christians to grow in your faith. Read your Bible and get to know God more. He doesn't just want you to acknowledge His existence. Even the demons do that. He wants a relationship with you.

Understand that when you place yourself in God's hand, your life belongs to Him. You must learn to sacrifice your own desires and submit to His will. You must allow Him to lead you and be willing to follow wherever He may lead. Your life won't get easier. Almost certainly, it will get harder. You might face persecution and ridicule. You might find that your friends desert you. But know that you are in good company. The suffering that you endure will be worth it when one day you stand before your Creator and He says to you, "Well done, My good and faithful servant." (Matthew 25:31 NIV)

REMEMBRANCES

After Dad's memorial service, I sent out an e-mail asking people who did not get a chance to share to send me their memories of Dad. I received these responses:

The one thing I would of shared---when we played cards on our Tuesday pitch day there was often times we needed another player & your mom would call your dad & he would come & fill in. Now how many men would join several ladies to play cards--I'm not sure he was always pleased but he did it!!!!

Alice

I guess my special memories of Jack would be of his beautiful gift of piano playing. I loved to hear him play. I remember one time when we went to Florida when they were living there and we went to a restaurant where Jack played the piano. I also remember his sweet and gentle spirit. Lowell will miss him at any of the LGH alumni functions. They were buddies for that.

Lowell and Joyce

Your folks were some of the very first people we met after we moved to Holdrege. JoAnn wanted me to learn to play bridge, which I never did, and set up a learning session with your mom and another lady whose name I can't remember. Her husband was a dentist in town and they were members of our church. During that morning's card game, your mom mentioned that she and your dad wanted to start a pinochle club and would Tom and I be interested. I said we would indeed. Very shortly after that, your folks came over to our house to show us how to play double-deck pinochle. As I'm sure you remember, that group met every month for the next 11 years or so. Great friendships developed because of our time together. I remember with great joy your dad's laugh as he set someone, and his groan as someone set him!

I also remember his love of music. At one time your folks were living in Des Moines, IA where your mom was a nurse with an organization that moved people where they needed temporary help. Tom and I were living in Omaha, so we drove over to hear a concert your dad put on. Tom wished he had brought his bass!

Your dad and Tom were always going to write the next great American novel. They had the first line written, but never could find anywhere to go with it. He was a gentle soul that I remember with great fondness.

Your folks stopped here a couple of years ago and we got to go out to lunch with them and play some cards afterwards. We took up right where we left off, and that is a true indication of deep friendship.

Blessings and peace,

Susan

If it's appropriate, you can add my remembrances of your father...
mostly in college, the many games of hearts we played, talking
sports, going to Red Sox games...and the last time we saw each
other, when he and Jackie visited us in New Hampshire, when
we visited the waterfall upstate and had such a great time. I can
still hear you laughing, Jack.

Terry

ABOUT THE AUTHOR

Julia Kercher holds a Master's degree in counseling and has worked as a mental health therapist for over ten years. She and her husband, Robert, have been married for eighteen years and have four children, Randal, Justin, Sheila, and Kiriana. The family resides in Lincoln, Nebraska where they are actively involved in their church.

If reading this book has impacted your life, Julia would love to hear from you. You may contact her at authorjuliakercher@gmail.com to tell her your story.

CPSIA information can be obtained at www.ICGtesting.com
Printed in the USA
LVOW070152301111

256972LV00001B/8/P